THE PHYSICIAN'S JOB-SEARCH Rx

Marketing Yourself for the Position You Want

Javad H. Kashani, M.D.
Wesley D. Allan, Ph.D.

John Wiley & Sons, Inc.

New York • Chichester • Weinheim • Brisbane • Singapore • Toronto

This book is printed on acid-free paper. ☉

Copyright © 1998 by Javad H. Kashani, Wesley D. Allan, and Kate Kelly. All rights reserved.

Published simultaneously in Canada.

Published by John Wiley & Sons, Inc.

No part of this publication may be reproduced, stored in a retrieval system or transmitted in any form or by any means, electronic, mechanical, photocopying, recording, scanning or otherwise, except as permitted under Sections 107 or 108 of the 1976 United States Copyright Act, without either the prior written permission of the Publisher, or authorization through payment of the appropriate per-copy fee to the Copyright Clearance Center, 222 Rosewood Drive, Danvers, MA 01923, (978) 750-8400, fax (978) 750-4744. Requests to the Publisher for permission should be addressed to the Permissions Department, John Wiley & Sons, Inc., 605 Third Avenue, New York, NY 10158-0012, (212) 850-6011, fax (212) 850-6008, e-Mail: PERMREQ@WILEY.COM.

This publication is designed to provide accurate and authoritative information in regard to the subject matter covered. It is sold with the understanding that the publisher is not engaged in rendering professional services. If legal, accounting, medical, psychological, or any other expert assistance is required, the services of a competent professional person should be sought.

Library of Congress Cataloging-in-Publication Data

Kashani, Javad H.
   The physician's job-search ℞ : marketing yourself for the
position you want / Javad H. Kashani, Wesley D. Allan.
     p. cm.
   Includes bibliographical references and index.
   ISBN 0-471-19336-4 (pbk. alk. paper)
   1. Physicians—Employment. 2. Employment interviewing. 3. Job
hunting. I. Allan, Wesley D. II. Title.
   R690.K345 1998
   610.69'52—dc21   97–38470

Printed in the United States of America

10 9 8 7 6 5 4 3 2 1

To Natalie, Brook, Nicole, and Ryan

ACKNOWLEDGMENTS

This book would not have been possible if it weren't for the extraordinary talents of a writer whose name does not appear on the cover page, Ms. Kate Kelly. In reality, she was not just a collaborating writer, but a master organizer and critical thinker who brought to the book a fresh perspective. I watched as she digested the material presented to her and magically organized the topics, added breadth, depth, and interest, and then refined each detail with the skill and patience of a master craftsperson. She is a true professional. We are proud to have worked with her and extend to her always our deepest gratitude.

A word of acknowledgment is also needed for Regina Ryan, as she provided the light for our journey. Although familiar with the process necessary for publishing research articles in professional medical journals, we quickly learned that we knew little about publishing a book commercially. Regina seemed to welcome the challenge and helped us find ways to make this book a reality. She introduced us to Kate, found a publisher, and offered advice along the way. For all your efforts, and especially your patient guidance, we thank you.

We also appreciate the efforts of everyone at John Wiley & Sons. P. J. Dempsey's enthusiastic interest in the book brought us to Wiley where we worked with Tom Miller and Chris Jackson, both of whom artfully helped to shape the content and make it the book we wanted it to be. As the manuscript went into production, Diane Aronson became the friendly voice at the end of the telephone who took care of all the details. We thank each of them, with an added thank-you to copy editor Jim R. Gullickson, whose careful attention to detail and thoughtful explanations of changes made the last aspect of the editing process a pleasure.

CONTENTS

Introduction		1

Part I Packaging Yourself for the Job Hunt 5

1 Getting Your Foot in the Door: Landing an Interview 7
2 The Basics of Interview Prep 13
3 Looking Good on the Outside: Acknowledging the Importance of Appearance 23
4 The Basic Interview 35
5 "A Group Interview With *How* Many?" What You Need to Know for a Panel Interview 57
6 "Let's Have Lunch!" The Art of Answering Questions While You Dine 63
7 The Ultimate Secret to the Successful Interview: Paying Attention to the Interviewer 69

Part II Special Groups, Special Interview Tactics 75

8 Getting Started: Internship/Residency Interviews 77
9 Getting Connected: Attending Physician Interviews 91
10 Practicing in All the Right Places: Interviewing for a Group Practice 99
11 Surviving the Managed Care Interview 105
12 "So You Want to Teach?" Faculty Position Interviews 113

13 Go to the Head of the Class:
   Directorship Interviews   123
14 Getting "Qualified":
   Preparing for Your Oral Exam in
   Your Field of Specialty   141

**Part III   Perfecting the Art
             of the Interview   151**

15 "I Didn't Say That, *Did* I?"
   Mistakes People Make When Interviewing   153
16 Avoiding the Sweaty Palms Syndrome:
   Managing Your Anxiety   159
17 Special Tips for Special Situations:
   Overcoming Possible Obstacles   171
18 Fielding the "Unaskable":
   What to Do When Your Interviewer Asks You
   Strange or Illegal Questions   183
19 The Politics of the Interview   191
20 After the Interview Process Is Over:
   "The Job Is Yours!" or "Next!"
   Moving on When a Particular
   Job Falls Through   195

Appendix A Preparing a Strong Curriculum Vitae   201
Appendix B Helping Others: Answering the Ultimate
            Question, "How Do I Get Into Med School?"   209
Selected Resources   217
Index   223

INTRODUCTION

If you're like most people, you'd like to have an interesting job doing work you enjoy while being paid well for your efforts. In recent years, that dream has been a little more difficult to capture for people in all types of careers, including medicine.

After over two decades of teaching in medical school while also maintaining an active consultative psychiatric practice with public and private agencies, I became concerned about the futures of some of the bright, eager, hardworking students I met as they came through medical school. As managed care has begun to change the way medicine is practiced over the last five years, there has been a gradual shift in the availability of jobs. It used to be relatively easy for physicians to get started. Now the career opportunities at all levels of medicine have become fewer, and as a result, students are faced with a worrisome situation. After 26 years of schooling (12 years of regular school, 4 years of college, 4 years of medical school, 4 years of a residency, and potentially 2 years of a fellowship), graduates may not be able to find a job!

As I thought about it, I felt that the one thing that was missing in medical school—where, of course, the emphasis must be on becoming the best doctor you can be—was information on marketing yourself. Because the job applicant pool is made up of many smart, hardworking competitors, the only thing candidates can do to give themselves a competitive edge is to borrow some marketing techniques from business and try to present themselves in the best light possible. What's more, I realized that this marketing approach would also help more experienced doctors who are looking to make a job switch.

In my work with medical students, I have become familiar with the questions they ask concerning getting a job. In addition, I am often called upon to sit on committees hiring new staff members, so I have seen both sides of the fence and felt well prepared to offer advice on how best to prepare for an interview. That's why I decided to write this book along with Wesley Allan, who brings to the project his hard work in investigating the topic and his own expertise as a mental health professional.

THERE ARE NO GUARANTEES, BUT . . .

While I can't promise you a job that starts tomorrow, what I can assure you is that getting your first job or moving up the career ladder in medicine is a perfectly possible task, but it takes some thought and some effort.

The Physician's Job-Search ℞ will take you through the process, starting with getting your first interview right through following up with a potential employer to find out if a decision has been made. Included throughout is a great deal of specific advice on how to interview for particular positions in medicine—anything from obtaining a residency to becoming a faculty member at a teaching hospital.

If you use *The Physician's Job-Search ℞* as your guide, you'll soon find yourself feeling confident about your future interviews, and you'll be well prepared to navigate your way through a successful job hunt, because whenever you're unsure what to do you'll know just where to look it up.

THE IMPORTANCE OF THE INTERVIEW

The personal interview is the single most important part of your job hunt, and that's why I've chosen to focus on it. The interview represents the first time the interviewer has the opportunity to really begin to understand who you are and how you think. You may look great on paper (in your curriculum vitae, or c.v.), but if he meets you and doesn't think you present well, then your excellent paper trail will take you nowhere.

If you arrive for your interview displaying that you are friendly, confident, capable, interested (and interesting), and a good doctor as well, you'll almost certainly survive to the final cut, and eventually one of the choice jobs will be yours.

HOW TO USE THIS BOOK

The first thing you ought to do after buying this book is read straight through part one. In this section of the book, we provide the fundamentals—what you need to know to get an interview and the basics of being interviewed, including the fine points of enduring a lunch interview (or any type of interview conducted during a meal) and a group interview.

While reading this section, you'll want to pause now and then to follow the advice offered within. Right off the bat, you're going to want to set up the job-hunting notebook described in chapter 1. This will help you keep everything you need organized. (As you continue through the process and go on several interviews, you'll find that many of the details tend to blur together. Your notebook will provide a helpful way of keeping everything straight.)

You'll also want to take some time to go shopping. Particularly if you're just finishing medical school, you're more likely to have in your closet a wardrobe of jeans and sandals or hiking boots than a business suit. While you don't need an extensive wardrobe, you need one terrific outfit to wear on your interviews, because *appearance does make a difference*. You'll also read about the importance of a good haircut. These are the types of grooming issues you might as well take care of in advance of your search. Then when the time comes for an interview, you're ready.

There's one other thing for which you should set aside time: Practice. People who interview well don't wing it. They've thought through potential questions (many of which are included in this book), and they've asked friends, family, and roommates to rehearse with them so that they are as comfortable as possible with the interview process.

As you begin rehearsing the interview experience, you'll find additional help in part two. This section of the book outlines the various requirements for all types of medical positions, starting with residencies and continuing on with jobs as attending physicians, HMO doctors, group practice physicians, and university faculty as well as directors, and there's special information on how to take a qualifying oral exam in your field of specialty. In this section, you need read only the chapters that are of interest to you.

Part three helps refine the interview process by providing strategies to help you avoid pitfalls along the way. For example, people inevitably make what they consider to be mistakes when interviewing, so we start with a chapter that sums up common mistakes and tells you what you can do to recover if something does go wrong.

Anxiety is a big issue when you *really* want a job, so managing your stress level is discussed in chapter 16. The remainder of the section discusses everything from how to best present yourself if you're a foreign-born applicant to what to do if the interviewer asks you an illegal question. How to follow up with a potential employer is also fully explained.

The appendix contains two important sections. There's helpful advice (as well as samples) on how to prepare a strong curriculum vitae, and there's a final appendix on what to tell others about getting into medical school. (Once you become a doctor, you'll soon find that this is important information to know!)

GETTING STARTED

You're at an exciting time of your life. You're embarking on a first career, or you've decided to make a career change, and this is your first step.

Like anything else, the more time and effort you put into the homework of getting a job, the better your results will be later on. By taking charge of the search, you'll find that you'll be in a position to choose your employment rather than waiting until an employer chooses you.

The best thing to do now is turn directly to chapter 1 and get started. I wish you well!

—Dr. Javad H. Kashani

PART ONE

PACKAGING YOURSELF FOR THE JOB HUNT

1

GETTING YOUR FOOT IN THE DOOR: LANDING AN INTERVIEW

If one of your parents is a physician or you know someone who became a physician 20 to 25 years ago, then you know that a great deal has changed in recent years. At that time, the old boy's network (even for some women) was an effective and efficient way to get a job. During their residency, young doctors would generally make enough contacts that a few phone calls would land them a job.

THE NEW PHYSICIAN JOB MARKET

Today the world is quite different. The impact of managed care has changed where physicians work as well as how they get jobs. If you're job-hunting in the 1990s, you have a broader array of places to work—you're no longer limited to a group or solo practice or a hospital-based job. Today you might still join a practice, work at a hospital, or teach, but you might also be hired by a managed care company or find yourself working in a for-profit, upscale walk-in clinic.

What's more, the specialty demands have changed. Today, for the first time in recent memory, generalists—internists and family practitioners—are in the greatest demand since they are the best trained for managed care work.

And despite some of the doom and gloom that's being written about career opportunities for the medical profession, here are some reasons that good physicians will always be needed:

Our population is aging. According to the Census Bureau, the number of Americans 65 years old or older will double from 35 million today to 70 million by the year 2030. And, of course, the older people get, the more likely they are to need medical care. Joint replacements, angioplasties, and cataract surgeries will be done more and more frequently.

The United States leads the world in health care, and one of the reasons is because of the emphasis on technology. As more medical breakthroughs occur, there will be a need for more specialists to oversee this advanced level of care.

Remember, too, that we have yet to wipe out disease. Unfortunately, AIDS, a rising cancer rate, and the challenge of drug-resistant viruses are a part of our society, and good doctors are needed to help combat these and other problems.

What's more, managed care is still so new that the consumer has not yet fully had his or her say. In all likelihood, there will be resistance to some of the more restrictive managed care programs and an increased demand for those that allow a bit more autonomy. This kind of shift will offer increased opportunities for new physicians.

There's also been a recent specific development in the physician's job market: Borrowing from the competitive world of business, there are now approximately 4,000 physician recruiters in the United States, according to the National Association of Physician Recruiters. In addition, the majority of hospitals have their own in-house recruiting firms. Certainly these new businesses wouldn't have cropped up if there wasn't a ripe job market.

THE IMPORTANCE OF MARKETING YOURSELF

Today's physician faces many exciting prospects, but you need to be more creative about finding the one that's right for you. You also need to borrow a page from the career seeker in business who already has had to learn about marketing herself for the business world. Because the job market is more competitive, you've got to do what you can to look like you're absolutely the right candidate for the job!

There's nothing difficult about marketing yourself. It's really nothing more than presenting yourself in the best light possible while also being aware of stressing why you match or fit in at a particular facility or organization. As you read *The Physician's Job-Search R̸*, you'll gain insight into the process as well as very specific tips to employ as you go about your job search.

ORGANIZING YOUR JOB SEARCH

An organized job hunt will be a successful job hunt. By taking the time now to set up a notebook for all your materials, you'll feel more in control of the process, and you'll be able to manage follow-up calls and letters—a part of the process that can be vital to getting the job. Here's what to do:

Purchase a standard-size loose-leaf binder, paper, and page dividers with pockets. The pockets will be the perfect place to put brochures and literature you acquire about the various facilities to which you're applying.

Use the page dividers to create five categories:

People. In this section, keep a running list of anyone who might help you with your job search.

Places. This is where you'll keep the names of the facilities, practices, or companies to which you expect to apply.

Interview prep. In this section, keep a complete list of questions you might be asked (and will want to practice answering), as well as questions you'd like to ask about the different places where you apply. (All this information will be explained later in the book.)

Letters sent. All letters and copies of applications should be clipped into this section.

Follow-up. This section is where you keep track of when and with whom you need to follow up.

If you don't already have one, you'll also want to purchase an answering machine. If a future employer tries to reach you by telephone, you're going to want to receive the message.

BUT HOW DO YOU GET THAT INTERVIEW?

When it comes to your actual job hunt, there are many avenues to pursue. Here are the best ways to start looking for a job:

1. Consider the timing. If you're in your last year of a residency or fellowship, you should begin your job hunt 10 to 12 months in advance of needing a job. If you're making a lateral move, you may have the luxury of not having to find a job under a deadline, but you should still set up a schedule for yourself so that you keep your job hunt moving along.
2. Make a list of everyone you know who might help you or have ideas as to where you might apply. People who work in the medical profession, the professors with whom you had good relationships, and recent graduates who have just gotten work are obvious sources for leads, but mention that you're job-hunting to anybody you think might be willing to help you. Your Aunt Hilda's physician may be looking for a new doctor to join his practice, or your medical school adviser may have just heard of something. Write down their names, addresses, and/or phone numbers. Over the next few months you should contact each of them and see what they recommend (or can do for you).
3. Read professional journals and study the ads. Each branch of medicine has at least one main journal, and there may also be specialty newspapers that publish job opportunities as well. Visit the nearest medical library to see what type of jobs are being advertised, and then start sending out your cover letter and curriculum vitae. This first round of letter writing will elicit basic information on the current jobs that are available at the various organizations, along with specifics as to what to do if one of them seems right for you. (See chapter 3 for information on writing a strong cover letter; consult Appendix A for examples of a c.v.)
4. Contact physician recruitment firms if you've finished your residency and any fellowship program you plan to attend. Because these firms have nationwide resources, they can be an excellent way to find out about jobs that are available once you've completed

your training. (Look in the medical journal for your specialty to find the ones that focus in your field.) For a fee (paid by the employer—not you), the recruitment firm reads innumerable résumés, checks references, and interviews candidates in an effort to find the right doctor for a particular opening. There is no charge to you for sending your information to them. If the firm feels you're the right doctor for a particular slot, they've obviously saved you a lot of time and effort. And, of course, if the job doesn't interest you, you can always say no.

5. Contact the state licensing board in any state in which you'd like to live. The board may have information on openings in their state. Also ask if there are any specific requirements you'll need for the board in order to obtain licensing in that state.

6. Go online. While this is not yet a substitute for reading ads and talking to personal contacts, there are now web sites that are specifically geared for recruiting people for health care jobs. Some sites even sponsor job fairs to allow prospective employees to submit applications online. While web sites are changing and being added all the time, one to try is Career Mosaic's Health Care Connection (http://www.careermosaic.com) where jobs for physicians, hospital administrators, nurses, and physical therapists are all posted. Also scout for job banks and electronic bulletin boards where job advertisements are posted. Software is available that allows you to target jobs according to industry, geography, position, company, and salary. And once online, you can fire off your c.v. via e-mail, speeding the chances of an early reply.

As in the business world, the personnel office is generally not the first stop on a physician's job hunt. As a matter of fact, it is virtually unheard of today. (The only exception to this is when an ad specifically directs you to the personnel office.)

While there are plenty of opportunities for doctors, there is one reality check you may need to face: When you're starting out, you may find that you'll need to go where the job is. The days of going home to practice, working in a popular major city, or settling permanently in the community where you did your residency training are becoming numbered. Today's graduates need to be flexible. As you gain experience, you'll likely be able to be far more particular in subsequent job hunts.

The ℞ for a Successful Job Hunt

- Don't hesitate to talk to anybody and everybody you know. Sometimes job leads come from the most surprising sources.
- Read the ads in professional journals and follow those leads.
- Check out ads for headhunters (physician recruiters) to see if they are looking for anyone with your expertise.
- Contact the state licensing boards for information about whether there are specific requirements for you to obtain a license in that particular state.
- Go online and visit medical career web sites for additional leads.
- Get organized by purchasing and setting up a notebook for your job search.

2

THE BASICS OF INTERVIEW PREP

For most people, going on a job interview is only slightly more fun than visiting the dentist to have a tooth filled. Even people who are generally confident feel nervous about interviewing for a job they really want or need. They worry:

- Will I measure up?
- What if I blow a question because of nerves?
- Will I be able to establish a rapport with the person interviewing me?
- How can I convey in a short time that I have a great background and can really do the job?

Part of the problem is that the interview process brings with it a lot of flaws. If you understand the special challenges that come with the process from the outset, it will make it easier to navigate successfully through future interviews.

THE INTERVIEW CHALLENGE

While interviews are a vital part of the job-search process, they are not an exact science. Some of the frustrating aspects of the process include the following:

1. **Interviews are an artificial situation.** While it would be nice to think of it as a "getting to know you" conversation between two

people, there is an unequal balance of power with the interviewer having the most strength. This inequality puts pressure on the interviewee to try to be pleasing, which may sometimes result in being false.

2. **Anxiety can interfere with an applicant's ability to respond to questions.** When you're nervous, it's difficult to present yourself in the best light, and there is always a tendency to try to give the answer you *think* the interviewer wants, not the one that really represents how you feel. When you're under pressure, it's also difficult to present a complex thought coherently.

3. **Some interviewers are untrained and do not sufficiently obtain the necessary information to determine if a candidate is qualified.** While someone in a personnel department may be experienced at conducting job interviews and will know exactly what he or she wants to elicit, many people who must do hiring don't really know how to conduct a proper interview. Even if an interviewer knows the qualities he or she would like to see in potential employees, it does not mean that he or she can structure an interview session to obtain this information.

4. **Interviews are rarely the same for all applicants, and the same interviewer may ask different questions of applicants for the same position.** Inevitably, questions will vary, and by late in the day the interviewer may be tired and is unlikely to ask questions that are as intriguing as those posed to other candidates earlier in the day.

5. **Interviewers may draw inaccurate conclusions based on the information received.** For example, if an applicant has always lived in small, rural communities, an interviewer may erroneously assume that the applicant would be unhappy living in a large metropolitan area. Similarly, if a candidate has little experience with a certain type of diagnostic equipment, for example, an interviewer may incorrectly presume that the applicant is unable or unwilling to learn those skills.

6. **Standard questions usually elicit standard answers, but the alternatives pose difficulties, too.** Standard questions that are almost always asked, such as "Why did you decide that you wanted to go to medical school and become a doctor?" or "Where do you see yourself in ten years?" may not provide much new or interest-

ing information. As a result, interviewers sometimes try to be clever and ask questions that will elicit unrehearsed responses. For example, a medical student might be asked, "If you could be a human heart or a human eye, which would you choose to be and why?" However, these fanciful questions can often unfairly throw off many candidates.

7. **Stereotypes come into play.** An interviewer may assume that a person who is attractive is more intelligent and works harder than a person who is overweight. Unfortunately, even intelligent and open-minded people often use stereotypes to help organize their thoughts.

8. **Biases exist in interviews.** For example, many interviewers fall victim to the Halo or Horn effect, whereby an applicant's single positive or negative attribute overshadows all other information collected.

The rest of this chapter will present and review some techniques that will help you present yourself well and overcome some of the difficulties presented by the interview situation itself.

The "Big Three"

Interviewers may ask you many questions during the interview. According to Martin Yate, author of *Knock 'em Dead With Great Answers to Tough Interview Questions,* there are, however, three primary questions that most interviewers want to be able to answer about each applicant:

1. **Able?** Is the applicant *able* to do the job? Does she possess the qualifications and background that will allow her to excel in this job? Does she have the motivation and work ethic that will enable her to do well?
2. **Willing?** Is the applicant *willing* to put in the time and effort to excel in this job. Numerous jobs and positions described in this book require many hours per week to keep up. For example, some physicians or residents commonly put in 80 or more hours a week. Thus, interviewers are looking for applicants who are willing to work hard and have strong character and drive.

> 3. **Manageable?** Is this applicant going to be *manageable?* Bosses want an employee who will work hard, but will also be manageable. Interviewers want to see someone who will be an independent worker, but who will also be a team player who easily accepts direction.

PRACTICE MAKES PERFECT

There are a good number of things you can practice in advance that will make an interview go more smoothly, and these techniques aren't something you can slap in place the day of the interview. They are techniques that require long-term thought and practice so that you will still be able to master them under pressure.

Speak Clearly

From your application packet, an interviewer will already know whether or not you possess the necessary credentials for the position. When the interviewer meets you, he or she wants to evaluate other qualities, including your interpersonal skills.

One of the most important basics of interview preparation is working on speaking and presenting yourself clearly. If an interviewer finds it difficult to understand what you are saying, she will assume that you always speak in this manner. In addition, if you do not speak clearly you may be perceived as being less articulate and intelligent.

Speaking clearly entails several different elements:

1. **Avoid saying "uhh" or "ahh" in between words and sentences.** Some people regularly fill in pauses in their speech with "uhh" or "ahh." The use of these phrases may be due to nervousness, bad habit, or many other reasons. However, repeating these phrases too often makes a person appear uncertain of herself and her abilities, and it may also make you seem less articulate. If necessary, have a friend or family member help you monitor your use of these phrases.
2. **Speak in an even and moderate tone.** Sometimes people talk very quietly when they are nervous. At other times, nervousness

manifests itself in a jittery voice. To combat both of these problems, try to talk in a voice that is slightly louder than you normally use in conversation. This slight increase in volume will help ensure that you are heard and help modulate and steady your voice. Have practice conversations with people with whom you feel comfortable. Tell them that you want to make sure that you are speaking loud enough and have them give you feedback on your performance.

3. **Avoid mumbling.** If you do mumble, this problem makes it difficult for other people to understand you. In particular, many people mumble when they are under stress or feel anxious. Even though this problem is common, mumbling makes a person appear to be uncertain and may be interpreted as a lack of assertiveness or competence. If mumbling is a particular problem for you, try to carefully plan out what you are going to say for a second before you begin speaking. Additionally, you may want to emphasize your lip movements. Be conscious of forming your lips correctly for each word. This process will give you added confidence in what you are saying and will alleviate mumbling. Finally, make sure that you carefully enunciate each word.

4. **Speak slowly.** Some people have the tendency to speak very quickly, and it can be difficult for an interviewer to keep up with what is being said. Practice slowing down your speech patterns. You'll likely recognize when you speed up, but you can also ask friends and family to signal to you when your speech pattern has become too rapid.

5. **Do not use bad language.** The use of off-color language should always be avoided during an interview. Breaking this habit—so that it is never used in a professional situation—is a goal you should adopt right away. Most interviewers view cursing as a sign of a lack of respect for them, lack of education or intelligence, or maybe even a lack of morals. In addition, some people are greatly offended by hearing curse words.

Definitions of what constitutes bad language vary from place to place and person to person, but always be conservative. Assume that using mildly profane words such as "damn" or "hell" may be offensive to the interviewer, and even if he or she should use a profanity, avoid using this language yourself.

Note: Our recommendations are suggested for people who do not normally have major problems with their speech. If you have a specific problem (e.g., stuttering) that makes it difficult for people to understand you, there are many sources to which you can turn. For example, you may want to consult a speech pathologist or speech therapist for help. In addition, one easy way to combat such a problem is to simply explain the problem at the beginning of the interview. Discussing your problem will make the interviewer aware of why you speak this way and make both of you feel more comfortable.

Ask Someone to Help You with Practice Interviews

If you're still in medical school or doing a residency, then you can practice with fellow students or your colleagues. If you've been away from school for a time or are applying for a higher position, a friend or spouse will surely run through questions with you.

Provide the person who has agreed to help you with a list of questions that you'd like to have them ask you. (To create this list, refer to chapter 4, "The Basic Interview," and note those that might trip you up.) Include on your list everything from the open-ended type of question ("Tell me about yourself") to the personally challenging ("Why would you want to practice medicine in a farm town like this?").

Encourage them to mix up the order and to throw in some of their own. Start any practice session from the moment you would enter the room and shake the interviewer's hand. This will help both of you take on your designated roles.

Afterward, ask your friend to critique the interview. What went well? What needs more work? Do they have any suggestions on how you might present yourself better?

Once is not enough. A tolerant friend will continue to practice with you over time, changing the questions and altering his or her demeanor (friendly? abrasive?) so that you have the opportunity to face different situations.

Ideally, it would be good if someone you know who has had experience conducting interviews could work with you for a time or two after you've practiced with friends and/or family. Think of someone in your field (a professor or someone with whom you've worked), and ask if they would be kind enough to help you out.

Like playing an instrument, you really do get better with practice.

Do Your Homework

While this will be discussed in more detail in chapters relating to specific job categories, keep in mind that once an interviewer agrees to see you, you have a lot of work to do.

Before your appointment you should find out everything you can about the organization so that you will seem knowledgeable when you attend the interview. While it is perfectly appropriate to ask an interviewer questions about the job, you should understand the basic nature of the organization and what its purpose is. For example, if you're applying to work for an HMO, you should know its primary customer base; if you'd like to be part of a group practice, you should find out everything you can about the group and what its specialty is.

Learning more about the organization may be as easy as phoning a friend who works there, or it may take a little more digging:

- Call friends to find out if they know someone who might have leads for you.
- Contact your school alumni office for names of people who might be helpful, depending on the organization and the locale. This may serve a double purpose. In addition to learning some information from the alum, you may actually find yourself with a friend in just the right place for putting in a good word for you.
- Many journals include descriptions of, or advertisements for, particular organizations (for example, the *Journal of the American Medical Association*).
- Check the Internet. If you belong to a network of physicians, send an open e-mail asking for information. Chances are you'll get a good number of replies.

Often, physicians must interview for jobs in communities with which they are unfamiliar. Because no employer wants to bring in someone who is going to be dissatisfied and move on, it is advisable to research the community to decide whether or not you could be happy there. If you've always lived in a city, you may find a rural community (with nearby skiing—your passion) something that you find very intriguing, or you may simply not be able to adjust to the thought of leaving the bright lights and the big city. While many job candidates do this thinking after they have been offered a job, the wise applicant will do it in advance in order to sell the organization on how happy he or she will be in this community. The fact that your cousins live 30 miles away, that you've always wanted to live somewhere where weekend mountain hiking was a realizable dream, or that being in a college community is something you find very exciting will help you get the job.

Most candidates who take the time to show a sincere interest in a position by doing their homework and really researching what life would be like in this new position have already moved toward the head of the class.

Stay Current

If you're interviewing for a job, you ought to know what's going on in your field. This may be as simple as keeping up with new announcements in the newspaper, or it may involve subscribing to specialty journals to stay up-to-date. If an interview question concerns something new that is happening in your field of specialty, you'll make a lot of points by showing that you're the type of applicant who stays on top of what's happening.

Make a habit of reading the daily newspaper as well. Small talk about something that happened in the news is very common, and you'll want to indicate that you're knowledgeable in many ways. If you've traveled for an interview, get up early enough to go to the hotel lobby and buy a local paper. It may provide you with some conversational material for your interview ("I read that the big ditch they are digging in town is going to be a Riverwalk. That will be wonderful for the community.").

Familiarity with the local paper will also give you an idea of what it might be like to live there—an evaluation you may need to make later on.

Count the Costs

One aspect of applying for positions that frequently is not addressed is the issue of cost. For many positions, cost may not be a factor because the institution to which you are applying will pay for airfare, hotel, and meals. However, this does not always happen. And if you're applying to a medical school, for an internship, or for an residency, you most likely will have to pick up the entire tab. In a research study published in the *Archives of Otolaryngology Head and Neck Surgery,* students seeking an otolaryngology residency position were polled, and it was determined that the average cost of the application and interview process was $2,403.41, with the range varying from a low of $500 to a high of $6,500. Undoubtedly, this figure will continue to rise over time.

For reasons of cost, it's a good idea to apply to places that are definitely of interest to you and places where you believe you have a reasonable chance of being received positively. If you are unsure about either of these issues, you may want to consider waiting and applying later. In order to help you plan for these expenses, here are some typical items for which you may have to pay:

1. When applying to a medical school, or for a residency or an internship, application costs themselves can mount up
2. Long-distance telephone calls to schedule the interviews
3. Interview clothes
4. Transportation costs, ranging from airfare to car rentals
5. Lodging
6. Meals during the trip

Costs: How to Manage

The cost of launching a full-scale assault for a position can be frighteningly high, and you'll be best prepared for it if you've planned ahead. Here are some suggestions:

- Medical students may be able to get a student loan to help cover costs.

- Some applicants (particularly those with minority status) may receive financial aid. Ask the site to which you have applied if such aid is available.
- Relatives may be willing to help you, as applying may be seen as a worthy endeavor. If you should accept help from family members, make sure that the terms of the loan or gift are carefully spelled out (e.g., are they expecting the loan to be repaid?) to prevent hard feelings later.

Avoid using your credit card to finance interviews. Once you get the position, you will have new expenses, such as moving, to take care of, and you'll be happier if you have no job-search debt hanging over you.

The Interview Prep ℞

- Accept the fact that an interview is an artificial situation, and do what you can to succeed despite the built-in flaws.
- Keep in mind that the interviewer wants to hire someone who is *able, willing,* and *manageable.*
- Practice speech patterns, speaking slowly and clearly to present yourself in the best light.
- Enlist help from others and ask them to help you practice being interviewed.
- Once you've been invited for an interview, learn all you can about the organization, the people, and the community.
- Stay current on local and national news so that you'll seem educated and will be able to participate in small talk.
- Interviewing for a job can be costly, so consider where the money will come from, and be somewhat selective about the places to which you apply.

3

LOOKING GOOD ON THE OUTSIDE: ACKNOWLEDGING THE IMPORTANCE OF APPEARANCE

While it's long been said that you "can't judge a book by its cover," we all know that first impressions really do count. Because jobs are tight and your competition is tough, you've got to do all you can to be certain not to give the interviewer any reason to think negatively of you. Anything from a smudged application to unkempt hair or a late arrival for your appointment can serve to turn off an interviewer.

For that reason, this chapter will focus on the importance of appearance—everything from your first approach by mail to your arrival at the interview.

CLEARING THE PAPER PATH: APPROACHING BY MAIL

If your first approach to the organization is by mail, you want your cover letter and curriculum vitae (see Appendix A) to make a great first impression. Whether your résumé ends up in the round file (the wastebasket) or in the "possible" pile will depend upon how well you sell yourself with this initial approach.

Purchase letterhead stationery, or devote some time to creating something attractive on the computer. Using letterhead (or the computer equivalent) that clearly states your name, address, and telephone number provides you with a professional-looking paper and serves the very practical purpose of spelling out clearly how and where an organization can get in touch with you.

The letter itself should be neat and clear. If you don't use a computer regularly, arrange to use one to send out your job-hunting letters.

Most important, the content of the letter should be personalized. You should express *why you're interested in a specific position* and *why you are particularly well suited to that job*. By highlighting these points for each organization to which you apply, your cover letter then serves as a perfect companion piece to your c.v., which by its very nature is not job specific.

Here's an example of a brief cover letter that a medical student seeking a residency might write.

Dear Dr. Smith:

I am very interested in the residence program at Lakeview Hospital. The excellence of your program, particularly for future rheumatologists, is well known, and I would be honored to be a part of it.

In addition to the training I have received in medical school, which included two rotations in rheumatology, I am very familiar with the problems of the elderly. For the past three summers I have worked at Sunnyside Nursing Home, so I am well aware of the complex combination of symptoms that can be present in older people and the challenges these multiple symptoms present to physicians. I look forward to being able to participate in a residency that will provide me with the necessary background in order to better help future patients.

Sincerely,

Christopher White

A strong, well-worded cover letter can be one of the best introductions you can have for a job.

In Brief

If you have seen a job advertised or know the specific requirements of a job, then you may want to create a different type of letter. In *Knock 'Em Dead with Great Answers to Tough Interview Questions,* author Martin Yate recommends the use of a type of cover letter he devised; he calls it the "executive briefing." To save an employer's time, an applicant can make a chart in his cover letter that portrays his qualifications side by side with the requirements of the job. The following example portrays an applicant who is applying for a medical directorship.

Dear Sir or Madam:

I am currently _____ and am very interested in the medical directorship job you have open right now because *(fill in with the reason why you really want the job—this is your moment to sell).*

As you can see from the following chart, my background is well suited to your basic requirements:

Current Requirements	My Experience
1) M.D. required	1) Received my M.D. from the University of Pennsylvania in 1984.
2) Directorship ability	2) Served as director of cardiology at Iopec Hospital for two years.
3) Ability to oversee hospital administration	3) Member of the executive committee for Iopec and Martell Hospitals for a total of four years.

I look forward to the opportunity to meet with you to hear more about what you had in mind in changing personnel, and I

would welcome the chance to discuss with you my thoughts on the position.
   Thank you for your consideration.

Sincerely,

Carole White

This format allows a potential employer to quickly scan your credentials to determine if you should be interviewed. Because you've carefully outlined the requirements, it shows that you considered them before you decided to apply, and the fact that you took the time to create an executive briefing also indicates that you are thoughtful (have a clear understanding of what they are looking for), conscientious (took the time to outline a letter specifically for this organization), and well organized (had the clarity of thought to compare background and requirements).

With luck, you'll soon be among the applicants whom they call for an interview.

NEATNESS COUNTS: FILLING OUT AN APPLICATION FORM

Reading your application form may be the initial contact the interviewer will have with you, and nothing is more irritating to busy people than to have to read an application with illegible handwriting, particularly given the number of applications that most hiring committees receive. Neatness may not be next to godliness, but it does show that you care about your work.

Make several copies of the application form in advance in case you make a mistake and need another copy.

To make your application easy to read, it is best to type it. (The stereotype of a physician with bad handwriting should be avoided at all costs right now.) Though obtaining access to a typewriter (as opposed to a computer) is becoming more and more difficult, it is worth some extra effort in order to present yourself in the best light possible.

If you're unable to gain access to a typewriter, you might consider replicating the application on the computer and filling out your responses. (This could be done with a simple application form.) Or you might even want to hire someone with superior printing to fill out your application for you. (One applicant with terrible handwriting actually got his mother to fill out his applications for him.) The last thing you want after all your years of study is for the person doing the hiring to barely glance at your application simply because it's too difficult to read.

HOW YOU LOOK = HOW THEY FEEL

Psychological research has consistently shown that there is a bias that favors physically attractive people. When someone arrives looking pulled together and attractive, they are perceived as exhibiting more positive personality traits than a less attractive person. Obviously, you want to do all you can to look terrific, and this can take some advance planning and preparation.

Dressing well will enable you to present yourself in a positive light and carry yourself with confidence. While self-expression through one's clothing is certainly the American way, this type of self-expression may work against you in a job interview—you don't want to stick out by wearing clothes that are too informal or too revealing. For a job interview, the art is selecting suitable attire that indicates that you fit in.

Dressing conservatively also helps to put you in the right frame of mind. When people dress formally and conservatively, they feel important and competent, and it also makes them feel more conscious of themselves and their actions.

For men, wearing a suit and tie is a must. Although these clothes may be an additional expense for those who do not already own a suit, it definitely is a prudent investment in your future. The suit should be traditional in cut and color. Navy blue and gray are frequently worn.

Some applicants opt to wear gray slacks and a navy blazer. While a suit is ideal, this is certainly an acceptable option.

A white or pale-colored dress shirt and a conservative tie should complete the outfit. When selecting your tie, you may want to follow current fashion to some degree, but avoid wild patterns or something that would make the interviewer say to a colleague, "Did you catch the tie that guy was wearing?" Being remembered for your neckwear does *not* get you off to a flying start. A power red tie with or without stripes is frequently favored by applicants.

Leather dress shoes, preferably black, are also necessary. Make sure that your shoes are clean and polished. A matching leather belt should also be worn.

For women, a dark (navy blue or gray are best) suit should be worn. Some females opt to wear pants, but it is recommended that a skirt be worn instead. It is safest to wear traditional clothing during an interview. (If you get the position, then you can start to show individuality in your choice of clothing.)

Make sure that the skirt is not too short, and be sure to check that you can sit down comfortably in it. (Position a chair in front of a mirror and test it out.) High heels, midheels, and flats are acceptable, but should be conservative in appearance.

Don't let the weather unduly influence your style of dress. For example, even though the weather may be warm and the temperature is 100 degrees, do not underdress. While you may want to carry your jacket until you come into the air conditioning, it is important to stick with normal business attire. A few hours of being a little warm is a good investment in making a positive impression for the future.

One job applicant interviewed at a graduate school in Fort Lauderdale, Florida, in early spring. The letter informing him of his interview indicated that the weather would be warm and applicants could dress casually. However, he chose to dress in a formal suit, even though it proved to be bothersome due to the heat. In contrast, another applicant decided to wear shorts and an informal shirt. Of course, it is obvious which candidate made the better appearance; despite having permission to dress more casually, the first candidate expressed his sincere desire for the position by dressing in a businesslike manner.

Overall, you want to give the impression that you always look as nice and presentable (i.e., conservative) as you do on interview day.

Putting Your Outfit to the Test

Be sure to try on your complete outfit several days before your first interview. You may find that the suit needs to be re-pressed or that there are loose threads hanging off the jacket. Women can also take the time to select stocking color in good light without the panic of getting ready. Once a color has been selected, make sure you have a spare pair (take it with you) in case of a snag.

This also offers you the opportunity to test your outfit for comfort. Business clothing needn't make you miserable, and you won't interview well if your collar is too tight or if some part of your outfit makes you itch. If it isn't comfortable, explore what you can do to improve the situation.

THE EXTRAS

While you needn't look like you just came from a hairstylist, both men and women should sport hairstyles that are neat and clean-cut. Women with long hair are advised to wear their hair up or tied back in a style that gives them a businesslike look.

Avoid wearing a great deal of jewelry. Watches, of course, are to be expected; and if you regularly wear rings, that's fine, too. However, wearing more than two rings should be avoided. Men with a pierced ear are advised to remove the earring before the interview. Women might want to wear earrings and a necklace, but all should be kept simple. (Pearl earrings and a matching necklace would be ideal.)

Women often ask whether they should carry a briefcase or a handbag or both. As a general rule, you want to pare down what you need to worry about at the interview. Imagine arriving for an interview and handling introductions with several staff members while trying to maneuver with both an attache case (or a briefcase) and a handbag; it can be awkward. If you prefer to carry an attaché case, use it to hold your purse items as well. If you do not plan to carry a briefcase, then select a compact purse that goes with your outfit. You will not project a professional image if you arrive with a mismatched tote that is worn out from daily use.

Obviously, you should shower, shave, brush your teeth, and take care of other hygiene needs (e.g., use deodorant) for your interview. Cologne, perfume, or aftershave should be used only minimally, because some people are allergic to such scents.

Gum chewing and smoking should be avoided. If you are a regular gum chewer, be sure to get rid of your gum before entering the building where you'll be interviewed; if you're a smoker, wait until after the interview to light up.

WHEN LONG-DISTANCE TRAVEL IS INVOLVED

If you are traveling to the interview, try on your interview clothes before you leave for your destination. As indicated, this lets you check for any problems before leaving home, and it also helps with your packing by documenting exactly what it is you want to have with you. Doing a trial run may remind you to pack an almost-forgotten belt or to pick up new socks before the interview.

If you'll be making more than one trip, make a packing checklist that includes each item of clothing that you want to take with you. Carefully press each article of clothing before departure, and pack carefully. As soon as you arrive at your hotel, unpack your bag and shake and hang your outfit. Many times wrinkles will hang out; however, take a travel iron with you for last-minute pressings.

Are you concerned that you have only one outfit about which you really feel terrific? Don't worry. You can duplicate your outfit for a return meeting with the same interviewer. People are unlikely to remember what you wore the last time, and by adding different accessories, you can change the look enough that no one will give it a thought.

CONFIRM YOUR INTERVIEW

At least a day in advance, call ahead and confirm the date, time, and location of your interview. Taking this step indicates that you are conscientious and like to be well organized, and it removes any worry on the part of the interviewer as to whether you will show. (Missing an interview, even inadvertently, reflects poorly on you.) This also serves the very practical purpose of allowing you to check that you have the right information and ask about any logistical information you may need. Be sure to verify exactly where you are going. Hospitals, medical complexes, and campuses can be overwhelmingly large and confusing, so it's always wise to get specific directions over the phone. If you're driving, ask where to park.

If you are unsure as to who will be interviewing you, ask the secretary when you call. Once you have this information, you can better prepare yourself by getting familiar with each interviewer ahead of time.

GET PLENTY OF SLEEP

Although you may be very nervous or excited about your interview, try to get plenty of sleep the night before. It is very difficult to answer interview questions if you are overtired and groggy. An ill-timed yawn during an interview can make you appear bored or disinterested in the position. Some extra sleep should let you bank the energy needed to present yourself in the best light.

You may find it harder to fall asleep because you're nervous, so plan a quiet evening with no major agenda—you'll discover that you're more relaxed at bedtime.

If you are in a new city, resist making big plans for the night before your interview. You may tell yourself that you will go back to your hotel early, but if you are having a good time, that may be a hard decision to make.

BE ON TIME

Make a point of being punctual. Few things will get you off to a poorer start than arriving late. One poor fellow arrived for a panel interview for a faculty position at what he thought was the correct time. He was very surprised when the secretary greeted him by asking, "Are you all right? We were so surprised that you didn't call to reschedule."

Confused, embarrassed, and angry, he then had a terrible realization: daylight savings had gone into effect over the weekend and he was an hour late. Most interviewers are very busy people, and lateness causes a problem for everyone. A tardy arrival may result in a shortened interview or, as in the above case, a lost job interview.

If you have a morning interview, set your alarm so that you'll have at least 15 minutes more than you expect you'll need. If you're staying in a hotel, ask for a wake-up call, but bring along a travel clock as well. Wake-up calls can be forgotten by the hotel staff, and if you've had a restless night, you may not wake with just one call.

If possible, plan for a few minutes of downtime before you leave, to read the newspaper (a good preinterview idea, anyway, in case something relevant to your field has made news), take a stroll, or just relax for a few moments so that you don't leave your home or hotel feeling like you've been on a treadmill getting ready.

To make sure that you arrive on time, you need to think through your travel time. If the interview is local (and more than a few minutes away), try making the trip at the same hour of the day as you'll need to for the interview. The drive that takes 15 minutes at noon may take a full half hour at rush hour, and a test run at the proper time will let you gauge your time properly.

If there is no opportunity for a test run, plan to leave early for the interview. That way you can manage bad traffic or take a wrong turn (even within a building!) without breaking into a sweat.

If you are in a new city, be sure to obtain a map and ask someone who is familiar with the city for directions.

If unforeseeable circumstances occur and you are unable to arrive on time (more than five minutes late), call ahead. In this case, the interviewer will at least know that you will be late and can rearrange his schedule if possible. (Don't be surprised if the interviewer puts you off to a completely different day or time.)

Ideally, you want to have a few minutes before your interview to compose yourself. This may involve locating a rest room, sitting down for a few minutes to review your notes, or simply having a few moments to collect your thoughts before the interview.

Be certain that you've found the exact location of your interview as soon as you arrive. You don't want to sit on a bench in the sun until it's time to go upstairs, only to discover that the room number you're seeking can only be accessed from a different elevator bank.

The ℞ for Making a Good First Impression

- A good impression from the outset is vital, and your initial letter introducing yourself or asking for an interview should be well planned and professional-looking.
- When you fill out an application form, do it as neatly as possible, preferably on a typewriter.
- Select your interview clothing carefully. Dress neatly and conservatively.
- Avoid lots of jewelry and keep accessories simple.
- Confirm your interview in advance.
- Get plenty of sleep the night before so that you'll be alert and look refreshed.
- Be on time for the interview! A late arrival can doom you from the start.

4

THE BASIC INTERVIEW

By the time you've been invited to come for an interview, you will have been through a lot of steps:

- You've sent a basic inquiry to the organization, university, or group practice that advertised that they were looking for candidates.
- You've reviewed the literature they sent you in response, and you've found that this sounds like a place where you'd love to work.
- You've sent your cover letter, c.v., and letters of recommendation to the person specified in the literature.
- You've been notified by someone that you've passed the screening process based on your credentials, and the organization would like to have you come for an interview! (The person who contacts you could be the chairperson of the search committee, the medical director, or any one of a number of people, depending on the organization.)
- You've responded to any and all phone or mail queries from them, and you've discussed and agreed to a date and location for the interview.
- Finally, you have received a confirmation letter or a telephone call that everything is in order for your upcoming appointment.

Now all you have to do is survive the interview!

An interview is an interesting process—while they are evaluating you, you'll be learning a lot about the organization as well as about the interview process itself. Here's what to keep in mind as you go through the experience.

THOSE FIRST MOMENTS

Entering an office or a conference room for an interview is often a difficult moment. How will you know where to sit? What if you slip or trip? If you're carrying something, what do you do with it? (Remember the advice about the handbag; carry as little as possible to ease your entry into the room.)

In all likelihood, a secretary will usher you into the room where you will have your interview. As you enter the room, try to walk confidently and convey a positive demeanor. When you are introduced to the interviewer, a good handshake and making eye contact are very important.

The Importance of the Handshake

Researchers (in a study reported in *Nursing*) have demonstrated the importance of shaking hands; a handshake is not only polite, but it also ensures that people are more likely to listen carefully to each other. Unfortunately, few people are taught how to shake hands properly. Some men use it as an opportunity to demonstrate their manliness by trying to have the firmest handshake; other applicants put forth a weak hand that doesn't really send the "I'm-glad-to-meet-you" message that it ought to convey.

A good handshake is firm and friendly. Practice your handshake with a friend or family member. Extend your hand, giving the other person's hand a firm (but not wrenching) shake. At the same time, you should smile, look directly into the other person's eyes, and say something friendly such as, "It is a pleasure to meet you, Mr. So-and-So." Using the person's name is a first step toward establishing personal rapport, and it also helps you recall the name by using it right away.

At the interview itself, the interviewer should extend his or her hand first. A few interviewers may prefer not to shake hands, particularly women who may have been taught a different etiquette in their childhood (there was actually a time when it was thought improper for women to shake hands). Let the interviewer have control over this matter, and should you encounter someone who chooses not to shake hands, then enter the room, and acknowledge the introduction with a nod of your head and "I'm glad to meet you, Mr. or Ms. So-and-So."

Demonstrate Good Eye Contact

Displaying appropriate eye contact is very important during an interview. It lets the interviewer know that you are listening and are interested in what he or she is saying.

Many interviewers think (perhaps erroneously) that people who do not look at them are disinterested, cold, or suspicious. While you needn't stare directly into their eyes every time you look at them, *you can focus on their lips or chin, which conveys the feeling of good eye contact.*

Often when an applicant is nervous, she or he fidgets and looks around nervously instead of talking directly to the person who is interviewing him or her. This is distracting to the interviewer and makes it difficult to focus on the discussion at hand. By sitting calmly and talking directly to the interviewer, you'll achieve the confident feeling that can help you get the job.

TAKE YOUR CUES FROM THE INTERVIEWER

From first introduction to final exit, let the interviewer be in charge of the time you spend together. It is he or she you want to please, so it's important to pick up on any cues the interviewer gives as to where to sit or when it's time to go.

A good example of following cues will come at the very beginning of the interview. If the chair in which you are to sit isn't obvious, the interviewer should indicate where you should sit—and by all means, don't actually sit down until told to do so (or until the interviewer herself sits down). While this in itself is a trivial point, waiting for these cues is indicative of good manners; it also is symbolic of the type of employee you will be—someone who will be appropriately deferential when necessary.

As the interview progresses, you should be equally alert to cues, both spoken and conveyed through body language. The interviewer will undoubtedly ask or signal when he would like to know more about something you've mentioned; by the same token, if you notice him glancing at his watch or quickly scanning the list of questions, you may want to be on the alert for specific clues to wrap up the discussion.

You'll get better at these signals with practice. A quick peek at a watch by the interviewer does not mean you should pick up your attaché case and beat a hasty retreat; it simply means you ought to be watching for time cues. For example, the interviewer may actually be enjoying your conversation very much, but wants to make certain he can afford the time to ask a few more questions; or he may be running late and wants to start asking some wrap-up questions.

SETTLING IN FOR A TALK

With luck, the designated interview chair will be a straight-backed chair in which almost anyone can sit comfortably and alertly. If you are unlucky and the chair provided is more like a low easy chair or a soft couch, sit forward in it so that you'll appear alert. This will also make it easier to get up. (Have you ever gotten into a too-low chair and then had to struggle to get your feet under you again? Not a good way to leave an interview!)

Sit with your back straight and your head held upright. Slouching makes you look like you lack energy and aren't interested in what is going on around you. Some people also interpret slouching as a sign of low self-esteem or poor upbringing. Both men and women should sit with legs together to give a proper and in-control demeanor. Later in the interview, as the discussion becomes more conversational in nature, you will likely become more relaxed and can certainly adjust your position accordingly.

SHOW RESPECT FOR THE INTERVIEWER

You absolutely must display respect for the interviewer. Even if he or she asks a dumb question, you should still take it very seriously. You will not receive a position if you exhibit any disrespect during the interview.

However, false flattery or being overly obsequious or saccharine in your approach is unnecessary. Believe it or not, the interviewer is looking for the true you, because she needs to be certain that you will fit into the organization. Follow your natural instincts and simply be polite and friendly.

While most people naturally have respect for people in positions of authority, here are some specific steps you can take to convey a positive attitude:

1. Be polite and display good manners.
2. Listen carefully and always allow the interviewer to finish speaking before you answer.
3. Do not dispute, refute, or argue with the interviewer's views or feelings.
4. Do not try to monopolize the interview session. Let the interviewer know that she is in control.

You must always remember that the interviewer is taking valuable time to see you. Any applicant who is rude or acts inappropriately will be downgraded immediately, simply because he or she has stolen valuable time from the interviewer. Keeping this thought in mind will help you exhibit respect.

100 PERCENT NATURAL

While chapter 2 pointed out the importance of practicing before any interview, the art in putting this practice to the test is to make it seem 100 percent natural—as though you never rehearsed at all!

Ideally, applicants should be familiar with most commonly asked questions (see specific sections later in the book for such questions). It is perfectly acceptable to prepare yourself with an arsenal of answers to questions that you think may be asked. However, try to make your answers sound spontaneous. Interviewers are also trying to see how quickly you think and react to difficult situations. Thus, if it looks or sounds like your answers are simply memorized, the answers will be less impressive. Methods of making memorized answers sound fresh include:

1. Look thoughtful by pausing for a moment to think through your answer. Don't wait too long, however, because then you may look indecisive.
2. Express mild surprise or bemusement when asked unusual questions.
3. Comment, "That's an interesting question," occasionally.

Sometimes applicants make it clear that a particular question is one they've encountered at other interviews. This is a poor idea. Most interviewers know that you must have applied to other places. However, they want to believe that their institution is the only one in which you are truly interested. Getting a job is a bit like carrying on a romance—you want the "beloved" to think that you are totally devoted to them.

(A LITTLE) SILENCE IS GOLDEN

Most people don't like silence. It makes them feel uncomfortable or awkward, so they try to fill the void by making small talk. Chattering about something (weather, traffic, your impressions of a new community) is unnecessary and can even hurt you. Relax and resist the urge to fill the silence—both you and the interviewer can use the time.

The interviewer may need a few moments to assess which line of questioning he or she wants to pursue. A period of silence also gives you the opportunity to observe any nonverbal cues and to evaluate whether or not you're missing something in the interview.

Small talk may also keep you from developing thoughtful replies to questions that are posed. Interviewers frequently ask very difficult questions, and unless you are exceedingly quick on your feet, you will need some time to formulate your answers. Those who answer too much off the top of their head may wind up saying something they'll regret. If you need it, take the extra time. It is better to be silent for a moment (or longer) rather than responding with an answer that is unsatisfactory.

HONESTY REALLY IS THE BEST POLICY

During an interview, you must be honest with the interviewer. Lying or embellishing on your experience is a fatal error, one for which you will suffer sooner or later.

In the first place, remember that interviewers will have read your application and may even have a copy of it with them. Thus, it's important that what you say is in agreement with what you've written on your application.

And while it may be tempting to expand upon your credentials verbally or on the application, don't fall prey to this temptation. Honesty is a matter not only of morals (i.e., it is wrong to be dishonest), but dishonesty can also get you into trouble. If an organization is serious about hiring you, they will check your references, and if you've exaggerated about aspects of your performance (e.g., duties performed, skills attained), it may be grounds for immediate disqualification. Or if you should obtain the position and the dishonesty is discovered later, you may be reprimanded or relieved of the position. Obviously, such a disaster could be exceedingly embarrassing and destructive for you and your career.

GOOD RAPPORT CAN GET YOU THE JOB

All of us have acquaintances about whom we've heard our own friends rave, but with whom we just don't connect. Mary and Matt may be perfectly lovely people, and you certainly can't find anything wrong with them, but you just don't get what people like about them. Each time you talk there's a tremendous gulf between you.

Well, you certainly don't want that feeling of distance or not clicking with a future employer. You need to work at developing a good rapport with your interviewer so that she feels comfortable talking to you.

That said, developing rapport is a difficult issue. Some people, particularly those who are more outgoing, seem to have a natural talent for developing a connection quickly. Most people, however, have to work hard to accomplish this task. Here are some ideas that might smooth the way for you:

1. **Remember the interviewer's name and use it frequently throughout the interview.** For example, say, "That's very interesting, Dr. Jones. Could you tell me more about your research?"
2. **Show interest in what the interviewer talks about and says.** Nod and indicate that you are listening and involved in the conversation.
3. **Ask questions,** particularly about the areas in which the interviewer has made comments.
4. **Smile when appropriate.** This makes you seem warm and helps you to avoid being perceived as aloof or withdrawn.
5. **Laugh when jokes are made.** A little laughter will help make you and the interviewer relax and enjoy the interview. However, heed these words of caution about humor in an interview: Let the jokes be told by others at a job interview. You don't want to be perceived as a clown, nor do you want them to judge you on your taste in humorous stories. Off-color jokes are absolutely off-limits; and yet, if you tell a clean joke and your interviewer loves dirty ones, he may decide you're too stiff for the job. Why raise an issue like this needlessly?

Developing rapport with the interviewer will make your interview proceed much more smoothly, and may pave the way to being invited back for another interview.

Friendly, but Not Too Friendly

The interviewer's job is to determine if you are qualified and desirable for the position to which you are applying. Clearly, the interviewer is not there to become your friend. Many people mistakenly assume that they should try to become friends with the interviewer in order to develop rapport. After all, most people would hire their friends, wouldn't they?

There is a fine line, however, between being open and friendly and doing what is perceived as sucking up. How to tell

> the difference? Express interest, ask thoughtful questions, follow the pointers given above regarding establishing rapport, and then leave it at that. If the other person doesn't respond to you at that point, there's not a lot you can do about it, and you wouldn't be happy working for him or her then anyway.

BEING A NAYSAYER GETS YOU NOTHING

No one wants to hire a complainer, so you will be well advised to put on a happy face.

Negativity often comes up in the most harmless of ways, but any sort of complaining sheds a poor light on you. Generally, what happens is that the applicant enters the room and the interviewer will open up a conversation with the innocuous question, "How was your trip?" Well, we all know how stressful travel can be, and so the applicant answers truthfully with stories of bad weather, missed connections, plane delays, and a poor hotel room. Unfortunately, this momentary lapse on the part of an applicant can immediately skew the interview; all of a sudden, the applicant is labeled a complainer.

No matter what travails you have experienced while traveling to the interview or in life, cast it in a positive light. A poor experience made into a rewarding experience speaks well of you. In addition, because travel complaints are so prevalent among applicants, here are some specifics for doing away with them.

1. Complain to people about your trip before you reach your final destination. Ideally, it is healthiest to discuss what's bothering you directly with the group involved (airline booking agent?) so that the problem can be resolved satisfactorily. If that isn't possible or practical, call a friend and air your frustrations before going into the interview.
2. Just before your interview, practice talking about your trip. (Almost every interviewer will make this type of small talk at some point during your interview.) Try to remember positive, funny

anecdotes that happened: you may have seen a famous person at the airport, or you may have found a really stimulating news story to read in a magazine you picked up at the airport so you hardly noticed the time.

You might also discuss previous trips you may have taken to this city. Relate to the interviewer some of your favorite places and fun things that you have done here. This also has the added benefit of expressing that if offered the job, you would look forward to moving to the community.

3. If you have never been to this city before, talk about how excited and eager you were to visit and mention some places you plan on visiting. You might mention how beautiful the city is (if it is) and the fact that everyone you have met has been very kind, courteous, or helpful.
4. If you truly had a terrible trip, and the weather has been so bad that the interviewer would know you were lying if you said it was fine, try to find one or two aspects that were all right—perhaps the airline was quite efficient at rebooking canceled flights, or maybe you met someone interesting while waiting out a snowstorm. Focus on the positive, even if most of the trip has been negative.
5. If you're under a lot of stress because of all the logistical mishaps you've just experienced, keep in mind that the interview will almost certainly be brief, and that you'll soon be on your way home or to a hotel room where you can relax and take a hot shower or a nap. What's more, you can tell your friends and relatives about your hideous trip without damaging your chances of getting a job or admission offer.

One final mistake many applicants make: they try to ingratiate themselves with one organization by complaining about people at another facility where they've interviewed. Bad idea.

First of all, remember this basic principle: This job interviewer wants to be your "one and only." Don't tell him or her all about your other experiences. Why should he spend much time on your application or interview if you keep reminding him he's just one of many?

In addition, don't ever criticize another person whom you've met in the job search. Communities of professionals are remarkably small, and the interviewer may know people at other places where you have interviewed. What's more, the interviewer may assume that you are a negative person and will go to your next interview and complain about him.

Overall, remember that interviewers want people to fill positions who are going to be upbeat and are basically easygoing. Nobody wants to work with someone who is going to be consistently negative or tense, so work on seeing your job-hunting life in a positive light.

EXCEL AT LISTENING

When you feel you're on the spot or being judged, one of the most difficult things to do is to listen carefully. Yet no skill will stand you in better stead when it comes to job-hunting. Applicants who have difficulty listening can totally miss a question and have to have it repeated, or they may launch into a stream of consciousness, hoping that by touching many bases they will at some point cover the one that was asked about. Some of the things that keep you from listening carefully are the following:

- You're planning what to say next rather than concentrating on exactly what is asked.
- You're rethinking what you should have said in answer to a previous question. (This one happens to all of us, and you just have to train yourself to remain focused on the present. You can replay the interview after you leave.)
- You become preoccupied with worrying about whether they like you.
- You feel overwhelmed by the situation or by the new information being presented to you about the job.
- You're too tired to focus clearly.

On a simplistic level, consider the following: A medical student applying for a residency is asked, "What was the worst thing about medical school?" Instead, the student hears, "What's the worst thing that ever happened to you?" Two very different questions—one is looking for a thoughtful comment about your recent experience in school, the other calls for an emotional response about something terrible that happened in your life. You can imagine the puzzlement of the interviewer if an applicant answers question number 2 when asked question number 1.

Obviously, good listening skills are important in an interview. Here's what you need to keep in mind:

- Try not to anticipate what the speaker will say.
- At intervals, try to paraphrase what has been said.
- Don't interrupt. Let others finish what they are saying.
- Pay attention to body language and other nonverbal signals.
- Ask questions if you're confused by something, but don't interrupt for insignificant details.
- Express interest by maintaining eye contact.
- If appropriate, don't hesitate to make a note or two about something the interviewer is telling you about the job. You don't want to make extensive notes while being interviewed, but writing down a few points stresses that you think what is being said is important.

EXPRESS INTEREST IN THE COMMUNITY

If you decide to accept the position for which you are applying, you will be there for a great deal of time. Even if you are only applying for an internship, you will still live in the area for at least one year. Thus, you should emphasize to the interviewer that you could be happy living there.

Familiarize yourself with the locality as much as possible before your visit. An almanac will provide details about most large cities. Smaller cities and towns may not be included, but they may be near a larger city that is discussed. Reading this information will provide information about the town's economy, weather, and other relevant data. You might also call the local chamber of commerce for information, or log on to the Internet and see what's available there. (Many towns now have their own web page.) Your job is to convince the interviewer that **you will adjust to the town.**

Many times, you may be applying to places that are geographically and culturally different from where you currently reside. Interviewers may ask you point-blank if you think this will pose a problem. One applicant lived in a large western city, Las Vegas, for most of his life. When he decided to apply to graduate programs in clinical psychology, he found that most of the schools that he preferred were located outside of the West. He was asked many times during various interviews if he thought that moving east would be overwhelming. He asserted that, in contrast, he was eager to explore new parts of the country and hoped to be able to move eastward. Indeed, he attained admission to schools that he liked and has since successfully transplanted himself to the Midwest.

Some specific ideas for showing that you will fit in include:

1. Emphasize the excitement of seeing and living in a new area.
2. If you have relatives nearby, talk about how nice it will be to live near Aunt Belinda and Uncle Bob.
3. Discuss unique aspects of the area that you might admire. For example, if the placement is in Florida or California, talk about how nice it will be to live in a sunny climate. Conversely, if the placement is in Colorado, talk about how much you like snow. However, don't stress your leisure time pursuits; remember that those in the medical profession, particularly at the beginning, are expected to work long hours, and you don't want to give the impression that snowboarding on the Colorado slopes will take precedence over emergency room work. Interviewers want to hear that you enjoy your leisure time, but they also want someone who is going to be dedicated to his job or studies.

"WHAT ARE YOUR WEAKNESSES?"

Because one of the most common questions posed to an applicant concerns his or her weaknesses, it is worth spending some time scripting what you are going to say. You want to develop an honest answer that doesn't cast you in a terrible light.

People are normally taught to emphasize their strengths and obscure their weaknesses. As a result, many people have a difficult time talking about their weaknesses. Some people may even become defensive if asked this question. However, bear in mind that asking about your weaknesses is not designed to undercut you. Instead, interviewers use it as a way to determine how self-aware and realistic you are. For the most part, people who are aware of their weaknesses generally work at trying to change them.

Most applicants use the old "I'm too wrapped up in my work" or "I'm a perfectionist" comment when this issue comes up. Although these are reasonable answers, they are a bit overused and clichéd. Most educated people have certain obsessive-compulsive tendencies; therefore, your response really isn't providing them with much insight beyond what they would expect from a strong applicant.

A possible twist on this that may work might involve discussing your own impatience when others fail to uphold their responsibilities. You might elaborate by mentioning that it's difficult to resist stepping in simply to solve the problem, but that you are fighting this tendency and are learning to use these situations as teaching opportunities. In this way you are demonstrating that, when a task is delegated to coworkers, they must finish it promptly.

Basically, there is no one right answer to this question, but obviously, some answers will definitely be more impressive to the interviewer than others. Here are some points to keep in mind as you consider what you might say in answer to this question:

- **Do** take some time to think through what some of your weaknesses are. Your answer should have some basis in reality.
- **Don't** refuse to answer, or indicate that you really can't think of one right now. That makes you seem uncooperative or pompous, and makes the interviewer feel foolish for having asked a question that you refuse to answer.
- **Don't** discuss extremely negative faults. You needn't confess that you have a tendency to procrastinate, are argumentative, have difficulty getting along with people, or drink too much! Discuss a less important and less serious flaw.
- **Do** cast your weaknesses as works in progress. You might mention that you are well aware of your weaknesses; however, you've always been taught to view them as areas in need of improvement. A

success story might follow: "In the past I have tended to be a little shy, but I have actively challenged myself in this area and think that I have made a lot of progress and have overcome this problem." This response shows the interviewer that you think about your weaknesses, but that you do not just accept them.

There's nothing wrong with admitting that you don't know everything, so another possible response to this question might be to comment that you're very curious about a specific specialty within your field (not an area for which the current position requires that you be knowledgeable!), and mention that because you would like to know more, you're considering a specific plan to gain the knowledge you need.

Remember that everyone has weaknesses. If you know what your weaknesses are, then you are more likely to be able to correct them. Relax and keep a sense of humor about yourself, and you should do fine.

"I Wish I'd Thought of That!"

We've all had the following experience:

The interviewer asks you a really perplexing question, and you basically blank out about what to say, but somehow something vague and noncommittal comes out of your mouth and you stumble through an answer. Then three questions later—your brain still mulling over the perplexing question—you realize exactly what you *should* have said. What to do? Backtrack. Try something like this.

"Excuse me, but I don't really think I fully answered a question you asked earlier. I'd like to clarify how I feel about _____."

An interviewer will be impressed that you had the clarity of mind to come back to something, and in all likelihood your new answer will be a substantial improvement on the original one. If you're lucky enough to think of what you should have said while you're still being interviewed, then there's no harm in going ahead and saying it.

THE GOOD STUFF: YOUR STRENGTHS

In addition to asking about your faults, most interviewers will also inquire about your strengths.

One way of presenting the best of you without seeming to brag is to frame your answer to indicate what other people think your strengths are. You might say, "Many of my friends have told me that they think I am very devoted to my work."

Employers like employees who are willing to work hard, so certainly one strength you might talk about is your penchant for hard work. Other good qualities that you could discuss include persistence, loyalty, and having a great desire to learn and gain new experiences.

Interviewers also want to hear what is *unique* about you. So try to come up with something that other applicants are less likely to mention.

One applicant who was applying for a position in the child track of a clinical psychology Ph.D. program started out by talking about being organized and persistent, but the interviewer kept dismissing every quality he mentioned as too much like what other applicants had said. Finally, after much probing, the applicant indicated that he had never met a child that he did not like.

"That is what makes you unique!" exclaimed the interviewer. As you can see, you may have to do a certain amount of soul searching to ascertain exactly what makes you different.

IN YOUR SPARE TIME . . .

When the interviewer turns to questions about your hobbies and how you spend your spare time, he or she is looking for a little more information about who you really are. While this is a time when you can basically talk openly about the things you enjoy doing, there are a couple of red flags you ought to keep in mind:

- If you're a closet romance reader or absolutely love watching television, these two hobbies are probably best left undisclosed. While there is nothing wrong with either activity, some people are judg-

mental about these types of pursuits (they consider romances a waste of time, and that television is for the uneducated masses, for example) and will think less of you for admitting to them. Better that you discuss the sports you play, the fact that you collect sheet music, or that you are an avid reader of current fiction.
- Don't make up a hobby because it sounds good. You may find the interest you mention is one shared by the interviewer, and if you're not somewhat knowledgeable, you'll be sorry you ever got into it.
- Don't mention a sport or a hobby that would be impossible to do in the area of the country in which the position is located. If your favorite activity is surfing, you may not want to mention it if you are being interviewed in Iowa. Or if you've been based in Manhattan and love Broadway shows, that's probably an interest you might skip when interviewing in a rural community. An interviewer may see a failed match between your hobbies and the resources of the area as a potential source for later dissatisfaction on your part.

Keep the discussion of your interests relatively brief unless the interviewer indicates that she would like for you to elaborate. If they are interested in knowing more, or comparing notes on golf courses with you, they'll let you know.

ENDING THE INTERVIEW

Often, interviewers have another appointment scheduled directly after your interview, so it is important to them that they finish your interview promptly and move on to the next one.

Look for cues that the interview is ending. One that is easy to recognize is when the interviewer asks, "Do you have any questions for me?" Though it's obvious that she's beginning to wrap up the interview, feel free to ask a few questions. Asking questions indicates that you are interested in the position and are actively processing the information that you have received. However, if the interviewer asks, "Do you have any *more* questions?" this is a subtle cue that the interviewer feels as though there has been enough give-and-take and that it's time to move on.

As the interview ends, don't sigh or jump up to leave the office as quickly as possible. Stand up gradually and gracefully to leave. Thank the interviewer by name (e.g., "Thank you, Dr. Johnson") and tell her how much you enjoyed meeting and talking to her. In addition, you may want to say something such as, "I hope to see you again." Such a statement shows that you are still interested, but also avoids sounding overconfident that you will get the position.

YOU'RE NEVER OFFSTAGE

From the moment you step on the premises until the moment you leave, you should be on. Don't let down your guard until you are safely away from the facility where you were interviewed. Keep interactions with everyone you come into contact with positive and upbeat. Frequently, you will have contact with secretaries and other staff members, and while they may seem inconsequential to many applicants, this is a mistaken judgment. An applicant who is polite and considerate may get a positive mention, and an applicant who is rude and domineering will almost certainly be reported. No one wants that type of personality around if it's avoidable.

If you meet staff members outside of the interview situation, it's a good idea to ask them how they like working there. Staff members are often some of the best sources of information about the general workings of an office or department. In addition, staff are also good contact sources after the interview is over.

In addition to the scheduled interviews, the interview session may include a variety of activities. For example, you may receive a tour of the facilities, have lunch with staff members and other candidates (see chapter 6), or stay overnight with a host. Always act appropriately. For example, limit alcoholic consumption when dining. Furthermore, an appropriate display of manners (e.g., opening doors for people; displaying good listening skills and good table manners) can have a surprisingly propitious effect on your overall image.

THE CHALLENGE OF BEING AN OVERNIGHT GUEST

If you're coming in from out of town for the interview, the group or organization may have arranged for you to stay with a host to help you save money. (Many medical schools try to find people who will host applicants overnight.)

If you are offered a place to stay, you should accept. While it does increase the stress of the trip because you must be on throughout the visit, it provides you with the opportunity to learn more about the people and the organization to which you are applying. (It goes without saying that you'll also save money.)

As always, be on your best behavior and offer to help your host with chores—cooking, cleaning up, and so forth. Offer to pay for expenses incurred by your visit, such as food or gasoline. Keep in mind that your host may be asked for her opinion or feedback concerning your behavior, and you want to give a favorable impression.

Most hosts will make an effort to provide some type of amusement, but be patient and wait for them to suggest something. Remember that your host is still actively involved in his or her world, and must keep up with her or his day-to-day responsibilities in addition to hosting you. Have something to read with you, and be prepared to spend some quiet time alone. The houseguest who expects to be entertained or shown around town will quickly become an annoyance to a host who has already put herself out just by offering overnight accommodations.

When your host is available, ask questions. He or she will be an excellent source of information about the position you are seeking.

After you leave, send a thank-you note to express your appreciation of her generosity and the trouble she went to during your stay.

TRY TO KEEP THE BALL IN YOUR COURT

Before you leave, make sure that you have an adequate understanding about what the next step will be. For example, some interviewers may tell you that they will make a decision in a week and will call you at that time. In this case, you would not want to call before that week was over to see whether you received the position. If you do call, you may be viewed as pushy or impatient, and this could damage your chances of receiving the position. In contrast, some interviewers may ask that you call by a certain date. If you miss this information or simply forget to call, this situation may be viewed as a lack of interest and someone else may be chosen for the position. If you leave and are not given any instructions, you may want to ask the secretary what will happen next.

ALWAYS SEND A THANK-YOU

After the interview is over and you have returned home, be sure that you send a thank-you note to your interviewer(s). Even if you think that you did not do well or did not like the position, send a note. You want to make sure that you maintain all possible contacts. You can never tell when you may meet your past interviewer again in another capacity.

The ℞ for a Successful Interview

- When introduced, start the interview with a firm and friendly handshake.
- Demonstrate good eye contact throughout the interview.
- Let the interviewer set the pace and be in charge.
- Be respectful and polite at all times.
- Don't be afraid of a lull in the conversation. Both interviewer and interviewee can use a pause here and there to collect their thoughts.
- Honesty in your interview is always the best policy.
- Try to establish rapport with the interviewer by being interested and tuned-in to the conversation.
- Don't complain about anything, and try to cast any possible negatives in a positive light.
- You'll be a better listener if you stay with the moment instead of anticipating or worrying about what you should have said.
- Express an interest in the community.

- Anticipate being asked about your weaknesses, and formulate an answer that is truthful without revealing major character flaws.
- Consider some of the qualities that make you unique, and be prepared to talk about them.
- If asked about your hobbies, keep the discussion of your outside interests relatively brief unless the interviewer indicates that he or she would like you to elaborate.

5

"A GROUP INTERVIEW WITH *HOW* MANY?" WHAT YOU NEED TO KNOW FOR A PANEL INTERVIEW

When you consider facing a battery of questions from a group of interviewers, it makes the simple one-on-one job interview look pretty simple, doesn't it?

The panel interview is primarily used for more senior-level jobs where there is a need for many people—it may be a search committee, a medical staff committee, or a group of organization leaders such as an executive committee—to meet and approve the candidate before he or she can be offered the job.

The thought of facing 2 to 10 strangers in a panel interview format is intimidating to almost everyone, and it does present the very real difficulty of not being able to establish a one-on-one relationship with any one member of the group. Instead, you need to take a different view of the experience and focus on giving a good performance.

And even though panel interviews can be anxiety provoking, there are benefits. One major advantage is that more than one person is now involved in the interview process, so there is less likelihood that your responses will be misinterpreted. And because the interviewers will likely assemble afterwards and discuss your interview, you no longer need worry that one individual holds your future in his or her hand. The final decision will be a collective opinion, so if one of the interviewers doesn't like you, his opinion will not be the only sentiment considered.

And here's a comforting thought: In general, the more people who are present for your panel interview, the more important the position is. So, if there are many interviewers, it's actually quite an honor. Here's how to survive it.

WHAT TO EXPECT

Typically, a panel interview will occur in a large conference room or other location that can seat a group of people. Sometimes, the interviewers may be seated in a semicircle with the applicant sitting facing them. It is easy to see how such a situation can make even very calm and composed applicants nervous! If you are fortunate, you will be seated at a table where you will be able to make some notes—a big help when facing more than one interviewer.

You will likely meet the people who will be interviewing you before you are seated. Acknowledge each person by shaking his hand, making eye contact, and smiling, nodding your head, or saying, "Hello," or, "It's nice to meet you."

After they have shown you to your seat, a chairperson for the committee may make a few introductory comments, and then he or she may pose the first few questions to you. After that you will encounter what is, of course, the unique aspect of a panel interview: the participation of multiple interviewers.

Because there are several people interviewing you, the dynamics of this interview will be very different from an individual interview. In addition to coping with a variety of personalities lobbing many different types of questions at you, the presence of so many individuals also changes the atmosphere. For example, there will be more distractions (foot shuffling, throat clearing) due to so many people, and some interviewers may not give you their full attention or they may be looking at documents during the interview. Try not to notice these interruptions, and don't take them personally. Even though everyone is not being attentive, this is normal and you are probably doing fine.

From your point of view, the interviewers are only interested in asking you questions to determine whether you should be given the position. Actually, much more is transpiring during the meeting. Because the interviewers are among their colleagues, they are often very focused on wanting to present themselves well. If they do not get along with each other or if it's a pressure-filled environment, they may be trying to impress each other with their questions. Actually, if you should pick up on this type of one-upmanship, consider this if you are offered a position there. If you have other options, you may prefer to work somewhere where the atmosphere isn't so competitive.

SURVIVAL TIPS

Panel interviews are challenging, but here are some surefire survival techniques:

- When you sit down, try to find a comfortable position and take a few deep breaths to help you relax.
- If possible, write down the name and position of each interviewer after you are seated. This will help you remember who is who, and it also gives you the information you need to send each member a personal thank-you note. (If you miss a name or two or spellings are a problem, check with a secretary after the interview.)
- Try to avoid seeming restless or fidgety.
- Be genuine. You are being scrutinized by many people, and if you are not sincere, it will be obvious to the panel, even more so than during an individual interview.
- The panel members will normally be well prepared and each interviewer will likely have preplanned questions to ask you. Since each will represent a different specialty or area of interest, this specialness among the interviewers will give you the foundation on which to build a rapport with each person in the room. For example, you might give a special nod to those in the room who likely encounter a certain type of situation you're describing to establish a you-know-what-I-mean type of camaraderie.
- Listen very carefully during the interview. Some interviewers may talk over the other interviewers or even interrupt them. Try to keep a mental note of incoming questions and address each person's query separately.

- Keep in mind that each person on the panel will have input into the decision process, so it's important to be pleasant and responsive to everyone.
- When you are asked a question, direct your answer to the person who has posed the question. If you know your answer will also be of significance to someone else at the table, you might address them as well. This permits you to target your answer to the appropriate individual, while also being inclusive of others from different departments or disciplines who may also be interested.
- Give equal attention and consideration to everyone on the panel. Sometimes candidates will focus on people whom they perceive to have more power than others in the room. This tactic is a mistake. In addition, interviewers who are good listeners will provide you with positive nonverbal feedback (e.g., smiling or nodding their head), which may provide encouragement to you during the interview.
- Don't be alarmed if you receive hard questions from certain interviewers. If you are asked a demanding or confrontational question, the interviewer has not developed a dislike for you and is probably not trying to trap you. He or she may simply be trying to impress the other people in the room. Just try to answer questions with a calm and logical response, and do not assume that it was a personal attack.

At the end of the interview, the chairperson may ask the last question and then make a few wrap-up comments. Normally, he or she will then ask if you have any questions for the panel. Make sure that you take advantage of this opportunity and ask a few questions. (If you do not ask any questions, you may look dull or seem disinterested in the position.) Unless everyone in the room seems to be enjoying a group discussion, hold your questions to two or three. If the group is tight on time, you don't want to be the one who caused them to be delayed.

What to ask? If you've been able to take a few notes during the interview, then you may have noted a few things that puzzled you. However, you can ask more general questions, as well. A suitable question might be, "What opportunities are available for staff to develop professionally?" or "In this position, in what ways would I be able to work with people from different disciplines?"

You can also use this occasion to point out things about the organization that you found impressive. For example, you could comment on the high level of camaraderie and professionalism of the staff. Or, you might bring up unique aspects of the facility.

End the interview by thanking the committee for their time and underscore your pleasure in being selected to interview for the job. You might mention that you are aware of how difficult it must have been for all of the interviewers to add you to their busy schedules.

Be sure to send thank-you notes afterwards.

Overall, the most important thing to remember during a panel interview is to stay calm and relaxed. Smile frequently to indicate that you are at ease, and be friendly and inclusive to all who are a part of the interview panel. By refusing to be intimidated by the situation, you will likely find that it's very stimulating to be a part of that type of discussion!

"So Tell Us About Yourself . . ."

After the introductions have been completed, you may be asked to spend a few minutes speaking about yourself. The purpose of having you discuss yourself is that the interviewers want to get to know you and hear about the important aspects of your life. *You should not respond by asking them what information they want.* The content of your response is totally up to you and will reveal your personality. However, the focus of your answer should be your best qualities and how they make you particularly well-suited for the job. Because this line of questioning is so typical you would be well-advised to work on a suitable reply.

Don't respond with a creative answer (e.g., "I was born in the house of a poor man . . ."). You can tell anecdotes, but keep them positive and as brief as possible. A long-winded story about losing your luggage at the airport on the way to the interview would be inappropriate. It tells them nothing about you and doesn't further your chances of getting the job. Stick to material that will be most relevant to your performance in the position. If you are given a time limit for your introduction, do not talk longer. You do not want to bore the panel before the questions have even begun.

The ℞ for Panels

- Most applicants are somewhat overwhelmed by the panel interview, so don't feel bad if you're a bit nervous. Everyone is, so you've got a level playing field.
- When introduced, acknowledge each interviewer and use their name. If you can, make some quick notes so that you can keep everyone straight.
- Take a few deep breaths at the beginning. This will help you feel more relaxed.
- Listen carefully so that your answers will be good ones.
- Address your answer directly to the person who asked the question.
- Think through what you will say if asked a general question such as "Tell us about yourself."
- Remain as calm and relaxed as you can throughout; this will help to assure that the interview goes well.

6

"LET'S HAVE LUNCH!" THE ART OF ANSWERING QUESTIONS WHILE YOU DINE

Because hiring a physician or medical executive or administrator is a very important decision, the interview process is rarely shorter than a day. (Even interviews for residency and fellowship programs tend to span a full day.) Sometimes the interviews even extend over a two-day period, so it is very common for an organization to take a candidate to lunch or dinner.

Sharing a meal serves the necessary function of eating, and it also offers the organization an opportunity to let a few key decision makers visit with the candidate under more normal circumstances. In all likelihood, you will have received an itinerary for your visit, and you may find that it specifies who will be taking you to lunch or dinner, and it may even specify the restaurant.

While the thought of being taken to lunch or dinner by the people you hope will be your future employers or coworkers may sound special at first, some applicants become nervous about it as the time draws nearer. They worry:

- "Am I dressed properly for the occasion?"
- "What if I spill something?"
- "What if they ask me a question when my mouth is full?"
- "How will I decide what to order?"
- "What if we don't have enough to talk about?"

While being nervous about being taken to lunch by your interviewers is perfectly normal, there is a benefit to having this type of interview—it's less formal. Talking casually gives you the occasion to show positive aspects of your personality, such as a sense of humor, empathy, conversational ability, or politeness.

Here are a few pointers to keep in mind that will make this situation easier—and maybe even quite pleasant.

LET'S HAVE LUNCH?

The lunch interview generally comes about for very practical reasons—you are in from out of town, and your interviewers are thoughtful enough to think of taking care of you through mealtime. Or perhaps you've been in an interview all morning and the group is hungry, so everyone moves on to lunch together.

Anytime you dine with prospective employers or members of a search committee, you should be aware that you are still on. What's more, the interviewer often looks forward to it because it gives him or her the opportunity to see you interact in a different, less formal situation.

The art of surviving (and enjoying) the lunch interview is to find a balance between being more proper than you would be with friends, but less formal than you were when interviewed in the office.

As for attire, if you've dressed as recommended in chapter 3, you should be fine for whatever level of restaurant they choose to take you—from a BBQ pit to a French bistro.

THINKING WITH YOUR HEAD INSTEAD OF YOUR STOMACH

Though it's always a nice treat to go out for a meal, this is a time when the food must take second place to the overall experience. (If it seems like a terrific restaurant, you can come back another time and eat anything and everything you want.) From the outset, you need to protect yourself from lunch interview disaster (spills, messy food, etc.) When ordering, consider:

- *Can I eat this without making a mess?* Spare ribs, a messy sandwich, and spaghetti-style pasta can be difficult to eat neatly, and the last thing you want is to spill food on your interview clothes.
- *Will this give me bad breath?* Having garlic or onion on your breath is undesirable because you may still have more people to meet, or you may be spending time with this group afterward.
- *Will I be able to eat this easily while carrying on a conversation?* Salads, pasta such as ziti or ravioli, a prepared chicken dish, or a casserole-style dish of some type are generally easy to eat without thinking much about it.

During this interview, it is imperative that you follow the cues of the interviewer(s). For example, do not order dessert unless he or she does—you don't want to be the only one at the table still eating.

Follow common table manners during the interview, regardless of the quality of the restaurant. Use your utensils at all times, and try to avoid using your hands to eat unless the food is clearly finger food, such as chicken wings or chips. Your napkin should be on your lap so that it will protect against spills and be handy if you need to mop up anything or wipe your face or hands.

Be sure to chew with your mouth closed, resist putting your elbows on the table or lounging in your seat, and do not talk with food in your mouth. If you are asked a question when you are chewing, politely indicate by holding up your hand that you will answer in a second. Also avoid chewing ice or rattling the ice around in your cup, as this can be annoying.

When the bill arrives, offer to pay for your meal. During some interviews, you may be expected to pay for your portion of the bill, but usually prospective employers will pick up the entire tab. In either case, thank the interviewer(s) and remark that you had an enjoyable time.

> **To Drink or Not to Drink?**
> **That Is the Question**
> Alcohol at an interview involving a meal is a tricky issue. For the most part, it's advisable not to drink while in these circumstances. You certainly want to be in top form throughout this experience, and if you're tired from travel or overly excited, the alcohol may affect you differently. However, if the interviewer is insistent, or everyone else at the table is ordering something, then you may feel odd not ordering a drink. However, once it's in front of you, drink lightly. You've done the socially acceptable thing of joining them in ordering a drink, but you certainly don't have to down much of it. (If water has not been served in advance, ask for a glass of water when you order your meal. Then you'll have something to drink instead of the alcoholic beverage.)

TALK, TALK, TALK?

What to talk about? In all likelihood, the formal interview is behind you, so you needn't (and shouldn't) repeat your experience or qualifications for the job unless the interviewer asks you specific questions.

This is a perfect time to bring up any questions that are still lingering in your mind. You may want to know more about the facility itself (its history, more about the population it serves, its philosophy), or you may have questions about the community. Remember to keep your questions neutral: "What are some of the recreational activities in the area?" "Tell me about the housing prices." "What can you tell me about the nursery schools for my daughter?" A blunt question such as "Where can I go skiing?" may lead the interviewer to think, "Oh, he doesn't want to come here—we don't have skiing nearby."

Otherwise, the meal is a great opportunity to learn more about your interviewers or future coworkers. One may have a fascinating hobby, or you may share a common undergraduate school with another. If you make a point of being interested in them, they will likely respond very well to you.

The daily newspaper also offers a great source of conversational topics. While discussing national news is certainly a possibility, you can also score big points if you've picked up a local newspaper earlier in the day and can ask questions about some of the stories that are occurring presently. Anything from a seasonal harvest festival to a bond issue that is coming up for a vote are topics about which you can ask questions. This also provides you with more information on what it might be like to live in a community such as the one you're visiting.

Unfortunately, some applicants make the mistake of relaxing *too* much during the lunch interview. For example, some applicants feel compelled to make jokes, brag about themselves, or use foul language because of the looser atmosphere, but this is definitely not a good idea. If you've always been the class clown, let them discover that later—much later, after they've grown to love the more serious side of your personality.

As with any aspect of the interview process, be prepared for the unexpected. One applicant who was applying to a graduate program was interviewed in the morning and was told to meet the interviewer at noon at a local restaurant. He was quite surprised when the interviewer arrived, bringing along his infant daughter. As a result, much of the conversation focused on childcare issues and developmental milestones. While the chaos of dining with a baby wasn't exactly what the applicant had in mind when he accepted the lunch invitation, he was careful to follow the interviewer's lead as to conversation topic, and left the lunch table having managed the experience successfully while learning a little more than he wanted to about "Little Sue."

While most applicants won't encounter baby Sue at lunchtime, you may find that your interviewer drinks too much, talks too much, or has some annoying habits. While any one of these qualities may be reasons you decide not to accept a job at this location, the challenge of interview day is to never reveal that you are anything but 100 percent enthusiastic. You want them to like you so that you will have the option of deciding which position is right for you.

JOINING IN ON THE "FUN"?

If you're spending the day at a facility, the organization will generally schedule a tour or another interview for you in the afternoon, but occasionally, some physicians like to conduct informal interviews on the golf course or tennis court. What to do? If you're comfortable with the sport, say yes and have a great time. And while you don't want to work at all costs to beat your opponent, you needn't hide your skills, either. Perform to your abilities, and don't throw a game—that in itself would be offensive to many interviewers.

If your athletic abilities are limited, you can still consent to participate in these activities. However, you might laughingly tell your interviewer that, although you enjoy this activity, you are still developing your skills. If you have never participated in the activity before, mention that you haven't, but are interested in learning and would appreciate a few pointers. Both of these comments open the door for the interviewer to set you up for a lesson with a pro (if he's the sort who really doesn't want anything to come between himself and his Wednesday afternoon tennis game) or to bring you along to give you a lesson himself.

Putting in a good effort will help you bond with the interviewer and also make you look like a hard worker and a general good sport.

The ℞ for a Great Lunch Interview

- Be aware that though the atmosphere may be more relaxed, you must still be on during this time.
- If you've dressed appropriately for the interview, then you'll be appropriately dressed for wherever your host takes you to eat.
- Follow the ordering cues of your host as to which courses to order.
- Use good judgment in ordering so that you don't find yourself facing a dish that is impossible to eat neatly.
- Order a drink only if the host is pressing you to do so. It's better not to drink at all during an interview.
- Use excellent table manners, and be polite at all times.
- The key to being a good conversationalist is expressing an interest in or asking questions about your host's activities.

7

THE ULTIMATE SECRET TO THE SUCCESSFUL INTERVIEW: PAYING ATTENTION TO THE INTERVIEWER

Here's any job-hunter's dream: You go on a job interview and encounter an experienced interviewer who knows the exact questions that will succinctly elicit information from you. The interviewer views her time with you as important, has read through your material just before your arrival, and will be very detailed in her interview. By answering her questions, you will automatically provide her with what she needs to know in order to decide you're right for the job.

But who ever encounters this type of ideal? In all likelihood, your interviewer is totally human, with all the distractions that befall all of us everyday: Maybe he got up on time, but the kids were slow getting ready for school, so that delayed his departure for work, and now here it is, 9 A.M., he's got this person sitting in his office expecting to be interviewed, and all he can think about is how he's got to get ready for the board meeting tomorrow. . . . Even interviewers are human, and you probably are not the only thing on the interviewer's mind when you walk through that office door.

For that reason, anything you can do to tune in to your interviewer will help you make a good impression. Think about it: As the interviewee, you are naturally focused on yourself. You are thinking about how nervous you are and how much you want the interview to go well and then be over. However, the interviewer is, quite naturally, thinking about himself, too, and may be mentally unprepared for this interview because of other things that are going on in his life.

Other issues may interfere as well: The interviewer may be new at conducting job interviews and may not even know what to ask. She may not be that knowledgeable about the job for which you are applying, and may not have had time to read through your biographical material, so that she is in fact winging it.

Or he may not feel well—a bad cold might make it a chilly reception for you. One candidate interviewing for medical school encountered an interviewer who looked very grumpy and unhappy. The interviewee could have been intimidated and easily done badly in the interview. Instead, she thought of a compassionate way to break the ice. She noted to the interviewer that it was late, and he must be tired from having to conduct interviews all day. The interviewer immediately brightened and said that as it happened, he wasn't feeling well today and was suffering from a sore throat. The interview completely turned around, and a pleasant conversation began because the interviewee thought of a kind way to ease into what could have been a difficult situation. The candidate is now a board-certified physician practicing at a major university.

Your challenge is to enter the interview situation, take a quick reading of any vibes that you get, and find a way to make sure the interview goes well.

Don't Take It Personally
Don't assume that the interviewer's mood is an indicator of his or her opinion of you. The interviewer may be having a bad day or be in a bad mood for a variety of reasons.

TUNING IN TO THE INTERVIEWER

The job candidate who can refine his or her interview techniques to include the following suggestions stands an excellent chance of being hired for the position:

- If this is a job you really want, then you're fortunate to be having the interview. When you are introduced, convey how happy you are to have this opportunity. If you seem genuinely pleased to be there, this will be well received by the interviewer.
- Don't feel the need to get the interview started immediately. Consider yourself a guest in the interviewer's office and wait for him or her to ask the first question and continue to set the pace.
- Don't rush in, presenting how right you are for the job.
- If the interviewer seems inexperienced, then quickly calculate what you think are the two or three most important points you want to convey about yourself during this interview. Then work these into the conversation. For example: "I noticed that the hospital serves a large Spanish-speaking population. I spent my junior year of college on an exchange program in Barcelona, so working here would be such a pleasure. I'd get to use the language again, and I know I would really enjoy the people."
- Don't be negative or complain about others. The interviewer does not want someone who is going to be cutthroat or a pain in the neck.
- Gauge each interviewer as an individual. An answer that may satisfy one may not be liked by another. For example, a family practitioner is likely not the person with whom to discuss your dreams of doing research.
- To a certain extent, you need to be entertaining, or at least prevent the interviewer from becoming bored. Being animated in your discussion will help keep the mood upbeat. You needn't tell jokes or be flippant, but liveliness will go far toward creating a positive interview. If liveliness doesn't come easily to you, practice changing the tone and the pace of your speech as you speak, adding inflection when appropriate. Smiling and making eye contact while talking will also help engage the interviewer.

Some interviewers may be quiet or not have much to say. Don't assume that she doesn't like you, it may just be who she is. If you're not getting much feedback and the questions are slow in coming, then expand your answers somewhat so that you provide good detail, but don't just keep talking. A taciturn interviewer will not warm to a chatterbox.

POSITIVE REINFORCEMENT IS PLEASURABLE AT ANY AGE

If you've done your homework, then you should also be aware of the interviewer's accomplishments, and it's wonderful to bring them up. You don't want to seem too saccharine or to be currying favor. However, if you're knowledgeable about the field and can comment sincerely, then it will be to your advantage to make note of something your interviewer has accomplished. The interviewer is just another person who wants positive reinforcement: "I was so pleased when I found I'd be meeting you, because I've frequently read your work in genetics."

STEERING GENTLY

Remember that you do have some control over your interview. The questions that you ask will determine the topic matter that is discussed. If there is a topic that you wish to discuss concerning your credentials, find a way of asking a related question. For example, if you are applying for residency and have an extensive background in research, ask the interviewer whether she is currently conducting any research.

Obviously, if there are topics that you wish to avoid, don't bring them up. Maybe the interviewer won't, either.

ASKING ADVICE CAN HELP YOU DOUBLY

Prior to leaving, it's always wise to ask for advice concerning the other people on your schedule. For example, you might smile and say, "Do you have any advice for when I talk to the chairperson or executive director?"

This serves you twofold. First, almost everyone enjoys giving their opinion on something. By consulting the interviewer, you've indicated that you respect and trust her judgment. Most people will be helpful to you and will enjoy being asked this type of question.

What's more, you may actually get some valuable guidance. You may learn that the director loves talking about a particular change that has recently been implemented, or you may find that the person you're about to see has difficulty hearing out of one ear, so it's best to position yourself so that you're on a particular side of him, especially if it's a mealtime interview.

Just remember that the interviewer is human and may have the same insecurities as you do. She may be nervous and want to present herself to you well. Likewise, she may not have much experience interviewing and may want the interview to go well. She may even fear looking foolish to you. Everyone wants to be liked and respected and to feel important.

If you approach the interview in this manner, always thinking of the interviewer as just another person, you will feel better about the entire process. In fact, you may even realize that you have much more control over the interview than you thought!

The ℞ for Ultimate Success

- As soon as you enter the room, try to tune in to the interviewer and pick up any vibes he or she may be sending (being rushed, not feeling well, etc.). This will help you manage the interview better.
- Don't take the interviewer's mood personally.
- If you encounter an inexperienced interviewer, consider which two or three points about yourself are the most important to convey.
- Be lively without being overly humorous.
- Be enthusiastic.
- Compliment the interviewer if possible.
- Ask advice if appropriate.

PART TWO

SPECIAL GROUPS, SPECIAL INTERVIEW TACTICS

8

GETTING STARTED: INTERNSHIP/RESIDENCY INTERVIEWS

As a med student, you know that your next step in becoming a full-fledged physician is obtaining a residency position—a task that is becoming harder and harder to do as the profession cuts back on openings. The American Medical Association has announced that they feel that the solution to the glut of physicians is to cut back—by as much as 20 percent—the number of students who continue on to residencies. Some states are even beginning to offer financial incentives to hospitals and facilities that agree to train fewer residents.

While there will always be thousands of openings for good students who present themselves well, this current news does increase the pressure on students to do all they can to manage the application and interview process well.

For an article that was published in the *American Journal of Physical Medicine and Rehabilitation,* authors J. A. DeLisa, S. S. Jain, and D. I. Campagnolo sent a questionnaire to all training directors in physical medicine and rehabilitation. The directors were asked to rank the importance of various aspects of the application process. The authors found that the most crucial factor in admission was the interview. For that reason, this chapter will focus largely on the interview process.

And what about fellowships after a residency? There's some information at the end of the chapter on those as well.

THE APPLICATION PROCESS FOR RESIDENCIES

The medical field has a very specific method for applying for residency. Most programs select residents via the National Residency Matching Program (NRMP). Under this system, seniors in medical school submit a list of their top choices for residency programs. A similar list is provided by residency program directors who interview candidates and then rank the applicants they think are best suited to their program. The NRMP then attempts to match applicants with programs, using both sets of rankings. A benefit to the system is that residency offers are spread all around, instead of one strong candidate receiving four or five offers while others have nothing.

Like anything else, understanding the system prepares you to work within it. For example, while the scattershot approach (applying to many programs, figuring you'll get in somewhere) can work, it's not as effective as a more directed search. In order to get a match, you need to demonstrate that a particular program is right for *you* and that you are particularly well-suited for *it*. For this reason, it makes sense to select programs carefully, based on the compatibility between your interests and the specialties explored by the faculty at the particular program. In this way, you are much more likely to receive an interview from a program with which you are compatible.

This approach will also save you time and money. Remember that you'll be filling out applications and going on interviews while carrying a full load during your fourth year of medical school. And typically, you will pay your own expenses to travel to any of your interviews, so you'll want to keep this process in the proper perspective. Most students don't have the time or the resources to make the application process into the full-time job it could be.

The application process begins by obtaining information from the programs in which you're interested, and putting together a strong application. Your application package will contain a variety of components, including your medical school grades, your achievements and accomplishments as noted on your transcript, the rotations you've had (such as surgery, pediatrics, neurology, etc.), letters of recommendation (including a letter from your dean), as well as a personal statement.

Creating a Strong Personal Statement

Your personal statement (also called a letter of intent) will generally be a response to questions posed by the program (usually 1 to 1.5 pages in length). In general, most schools will be looking for the reasons why you want to enter their program and why you want to pursue the field of medicine you've chosen. Your statement will be read by interviewers as well as others on the residency selection committee, and it is your first opportunity to show them what a good match you will be.

As soon as you receive the application, read through the entire document; you can do this without feeling nervous, because there is no need to fill it out right away. Once you've read the specific questions posed by the program for the personal statement, you can mull them over for a time before having to answer them. You'll be surprised how this will help you. (Too many times, applicants worry that they will be overwhelmed by writer's block, so they procrastinate and don't even read the questions until the deadline is upon them. This is a mistake.)

Dedicate a loose-leaf binder to your application process, and create a page (at least one per program) for jotting down thoughts you have as to how you'd like to answer the questions. That way you'll likely have a full set of notes created when you sit down to actually write your statement.

Give yourself a deadline for writing the statement. Select a date far enough ahead of time so that you can put the finished application aside for a week and then reread and reedit it. As you write, keep checking back to the application form, and be careful to answer the exact questions that are asked as specifically as possible.

Focus on carefully matching your stated goals and aspirations with the programs to which you are applying. When the committee finishes reading your application, you want them to be thinking, "Boy, this is a good candidate for us."

When you have finished a draft of your statement, give it to someone else (perhaps a trusted professor) and have him or her read the letter for content as well as grammatical errors. In fact, have several people read and comment on your letter, if possible.

Once you are satisfied that you've given it your best effort, print out a clean copy to put with the rest of the application information.

Letters of Recommendation

Letters of recommendation are also important in the admission process. Yet deciding upon whom you should ask to write a letter for you, and then working up the nerve to actually ask them, is a job in itself. However, by following these guidelines, you make this a relatively painless part of the process.

Who do I ask? Most programs require three letters of recommendation from relevant faculty members who can convey that they really know you and your qualifications. With luck, these people will be able to bring life and perspective to your application.

While department rank is not vital, it doesn't hurt either, so for one of your letters select the highest-ranking person in your department of specialty who you feel knows you well (and likes your work).

Letters of recommendation generally do not come from personal or family friends, family members, your religious leader, your therapist, or your personal physician. The only time these people would be appropriate is if one of them has an incredible story to tell about you, one that only he or she could tell. For example, if you've overcome a learning disability to get to where you are, or if you suffered some incredible setback and still managed to achieve all that you have, letters from those who witnessed your experience might be stronger than someone who can speak of you only in the context of medical school.

When do I ask? Ask early. Look carefully at the due dates for your applications and ask for a letter of recommendation at least one month prior to the earliest deadline. Most faculty members will receive a multitude of requests from students and will appreciate having as much time as possible.

How do I ask? When you first approach the faculty member, ask if he or she would be comfortable and willing to write a letter for you. That way, the prospective letter writer will not feel pressured into the task and can refuse if he does not think that he can write a favorable letter for you. If you have doubts about the contents of the letter that the person may write, be frank. Ask the person, "Do you think that you can write a strong letter of recommendation for me?" Asking such a direct question may be difficult, but you must balance this relatively minor discomfort against the prospect of not receiving admission to the program that you admire due to a poor letter of recommendation.

Create a letter-writing packet for the letter writer. Make a folder that neatly includes the application form for each program to which you are applying. Include preaddressed stamped envelopes. Many schools request that certain questions be answered that are included on a specific form. Also, include a copy of your curriculum vitae (see Appendix A), transcripts, a personal statement, a list of programs to which you are applying, and the deadlines for each program. Make it as easy as possible for the letter writer to write the letter and send it on time.

Take the time to think through your request and be very specific about what you need. Writing letters of recommendation for students is part of a faculty member's job. However, letter writing is a time-consuming process, so anything you can do to make the process as easy as possible for those from whom you request letters will be appreciated.

Following up. Approximately two weeks before the final due date, call the secretary at the school to confirm that the letters have arrived. At this time, you can also check to see if other application materials have arrived.

If the deadline is approaching and your letters have not arrived at the residency program, do not hesitate to remind the faculty members that the letters are due soon. Of course, try to put your reminders in a nonthreatening and non-nagging manner. You may phrase them as: "Thanks again for agreeing to write my letters of recommendation. I also wanted to remind you that they are due soon."

Although most programs have a system to let you know that your application is complete, some may not; so if you haven't heard, it's okay to call. (The secretary is a vital person for you right now; be polite.) At that point you can ask about an interview date as well.

INTERVIEW PREP: DO YOUR HOMEWORK

A recent study published in *Academic Medicine* examining the interview techniques used by residency programs in family practice showed that most interviewers (69 percent) utilize an unstructured and thus unstandardized interview method. So while no one can tell you exactly what to expect during an interview, there are steps you can take in an effort to do the best you can with the experience.

Once the interview is scheduled, you need to do your homework. Call the secretary to try to find out with whom you will be interviewing. (This information may not actually be available until a few days before the interview date.)

Many sites will provide you with a pamphlet that discusses each faculty member and his or her interests. Read about what kind of work and/or research the interviewer does. If the interviewer has published articles or books, read some of these materials to familiarize yourself with them. When the interviewer is conversing about his or her work, you will want to be able to ask intelligent and thoughtful questions. If you already have prior knowledge concerning this work, asking questions and expressing interest is a much easier task.

In addition, you should familiarize yourself with the residency training director; his or her interests and philosophies will have a major impact on the residency program. What's more, the training director is usually a very important person at the site and may have a great deal of input into the admissions process.

Most libraries will have directories that list medical residency sites and give information about their training directors.

THE INTERVIEW

Just as you presented your compatibility with the program in your personal statement, the interview is the time to personally demonstrate to the interviewer how well you fit with the program. The interviewer wants students who have similar views and an orientation that matches the outlook of the program.

Indeed, one study of residency programs for physical medicine and rehabilitation (published in the *American Journal of Physical Medicine and Rehabilitation*) found that displaying compatibility with the program during the interview was the single most important factor in obtaining admission. Look at the results of 15 factors that come up during an interview and their ranking in importance:

Characteristic	Mean Ranking
1. Compatibility with program	4.4
2. Ability to articulate thoughts	4.2
3. Ability to work with the team	4.2
4. Ability to listen	4.1
5. Commitment to hard work	4.1
6. Ability to grow in knowledge	4.1
7. Maturity	3.9
8. Ability to solve problems	3.9
9. Fund of medical knowledge	3.8
10. Sensitivity to others' psychosocial needs	3.7
11. Relevant questions asked	3.7
12. Personal appearance and professionalism	3.6
13. Level of confidence	3.6
14. Realistic self-appraisal	3.6
15. Knowledge of the specialty	3.5

This list also provides an excellent summation of some of the other qualities that interviewers are looking for. Think carefully about how you exhibit these characteristics in everyday social interactions. Then, think about how you might be able to demonstrate these qualities during an interview procedure.

Here are some suggested ways to be among those candidates whom the committee views positively.

Be Enthusiastic

Above all, you want to convey excitement and enthusiasm for this next stage of training. Some people come to the interview and seem to view residency simply as a hurdle that *has* to be completed to finish their training. They see it only as a means to an end—not a popular thought to convey to your interviewers, who are working hard to create or maintain a strong residency program.

Interviewers want to believe that you want to do a residency at their program because you have an inherent interest in what you do and want to develop and calibrate your skills. Show them that you are enthusiastic about learning and about completing a residency. Stress the fact that residency is an opportunity for you to learn and later on to help people and become more proficient in what you do. Emphasize that you enjoy learning and think that you can learn a great deal from the experiences you will encounter at the program and from the faculty.

When With Adults, Think Like an Adult

Most people who are applying for residency are in their mid twenties and may thus still feel like young college students. However, you are now at the point in your academic career when working hard should be your first priority. Although you may still see yourself as a carefree college student, you will no longer be so if you receive admission to a program as a house officer (another name for intern or resident). Present yourself during the interview as responsible and thoughtful. Residency programs do not want to admit someone who parties too hard or is going to be a troublemaker.

When it comes to your student lifestyle, be selective. If you organized a sit-in at the dean's office, you needn't bring this up at your interview. Also, do not talk about any wild behaviors you may engage in, such as excessive drinking or partying. These behaviors may be acceptable during college, but interviewers at these programs want someone who displays adult sensibilities. Show that you like to cooperate and act like a responsible adult.

Display Strong Organizational Skills

Bring with you a copy of your curriculum vitae and letter of intent as well as any other supporting documents you included in your application. Organize all of these materials carefully in a folder, along with a pad of paper and a writing utensil to take notes.

This folder can also be used to hold documents that you will be given during your interview. For example, some interviewers might give you copies of reprints of their articles or manuscripts that they are working on at the time. Bringing a folder will allow you to file away all of these materials so that you do not have to worry about carrying or losing them during your interviews. Good organizational skills are always a positive trait and will be viewed positively by interviewers.

THE VITAL QUESTION: "WHY DO YOU WANT TO DO YOUR RESIDENCY HERE?"

Interviewers almost always ask candidates why they have chosen to apply to this particular program. This question is one that an applicant must have a clear idea how to answer. Therefore, you want to think about the unique aspects of the program that influenced you to apply there. In your answer, you should specifically:

1. Emphasize the unique experiences that the program will give you.
2. Talk about faculty or staff members with whom you would like to work.
3. Talk about unique treatments, assessments, or procedures that the program provides.
4. Indicate other acceptable reasons, including (*a*) I like the attractions of the program, (*b*) the site is close to my family or the family of my spouse, (*c*) other residents seem happy here, or (*d*) I like the city.

ASK GOOD QUESTIONS

At the end of the interview, most interviewers will ask you if you have any questions. Be sure to have some prepared, as this is one way you have to convey your interest and enthusiasm for the program. (Not asking questions at this time will make you appear to be disinterested or even dull.) This is also your best chance to learn more about the program so that you'll have more information for deciding whether it's the program for you. Here are some sample questions that may help you think of additional ones of your own:

1. What kind of research is currently being conducted in this department?
2. How much direct supervision do most faculty members provide to trainees?
3. How much direct responsibility are residents allowed to have for patients?
4. What kind of caseload are most residents expected to have?
5. Do most residents from this program pass their boards?
6. What kinds of fellowships do most people find when they complete their placement at this program?
7. What percentage of residents go into academia? Research?

Before you leave the interview, you should make sure that you have asked the questions that are a top priority to you. After all, the interview may be the only opportunity to gather the information you need to decide whether you will accept an offer from this program.

EXPLORE THE SITE

Most residency programs arrange for you to have a guided tour of the site. This will allow you to see all of the facility and the school, not just those emphasized by the department.

The person appointed to show you around will likely introduce you to people as you go. It is important that you maintain an eager and interested appearance at all times. Remember that the interview is a continuous process. Even if the atmosphere becomes more casual, you are still being interviewed.

Arrangements are often made for applicants to have lunch with current residents. These residents may, in fact, be your most valuable resource concerning information about the program. It is particularly important that you talk to house officers and assess their satisfaction.
A. C. Simmonds, J. M. Robbins, M. R. Brinker, J. C. Rice, and M. D.

Kerstein (authors of an article that appeared in *Academic Medicine*) report that prospective residents frequently stated that house officer satisfaction with a program was the most important factor in the choice of that program.

Others have found that many students seeking admission to a residency program rated resident satisfaction with the program to be the single most important criteria for selecting a position. Thus, you want to ask concise questions that will elicit whether the residents are happy with the program. Some questions that you may want to ask the house officers and other trainees include:

1. What do you think of the quality of the faculty?
2. How satisfied are you with the program?
3. What is a typical day like for you in this program?
4. What is your clinical/patient caseload like?
5. What do you think is the quality of other residents in the program?
6. How much contact do you have with faculty members?
7. How much direct supervision do you receive?
8. What kind of research opportunities are available for house officers?
9. What is the typical relationship between residents and faculty?
10. Would you choose this program if you could make your choice over again?
11. What kind of opportunities are there for socializing with other residents?
12. What are living conditions like for most residents?
13. How stable is the faculty? Do most faculty stay here long?
14. How much positive or constructive feedback is normally provided to residents by faculty?
15. What kind of on-call schedules do most house officers have?

Most interns and residents will be eager to talk about themselves and the program, and are likely to give you some straightforward feedback. So use this opportunity as a valuable resource to learn more about the site.

You might also like to take time to explore the facilities on your own.

HAPPY IN YOUR WORK, HAPPY IN YOUR LIFE

Many people refer to the residency period as "trial by fire." Indeed, most doctors can attest to the extreme pressure that accompanies such a position. For this reason, it's important to be cautious and heads-up when evaluating programs. You don't want to put as your first match a place that will ultimately be wrong for you.

One issue to watch carefully is the nature of the training provided. It is vital that a program view the *proper training* of future physicians as their mission, rather than using residents as an inexpensive way to find badly needed extra help at the facility. Unfortunately, some programs look for hard workers who can help faculty or staff fulfill their duties, and you may spend much of your time completing repetitive tasks (e.g., physical or neurological examinations). While practical experience and on-the-job learning does present benefits, a good program will have careful monitoring of your work and will put the emphasis on teaching. The first time you are on call, you will be thrown into action with little experience, and you will be expected to fulfill laborious and potentially overwhelming duties. It is important that the program has prepared you for the work as well as the pressure.

You should consider the following:

1. Make sure that you get full information concerning the training that you will receive. From this information, you can decide if this program would be a good experience for you. Remember, you do not want to enter a stressful, high-pressure situation and receive inadequate training.
2. Ask the house officers for details about the program. Although most persons currently serving as interns or residents will try to be positive about the program, much information can still be gained. Even if positive information is being shared, look for signs of hesitancy (e.g., pauses, searching for words) that may indicate that the resident is being cautious.

Your residency choice is an important one, not only in terms of training, but also in gaining experience and contacts for future employment. Do the best you can to present yourself well so that ultimately, you feel that your match is a really good fit. Good luck.

FELLOWSHIP INTERVIEWS

Obtaining a subspecialty is something worth thinking about even in this day of managed care, when there is a strong preference for generalists. However, the number of positions available for fellowships is decreasing, making these programs more and more competitive.

A good reason for continuing with a fellowship is that it makes you more desirable in the job market because you have additional expertise. If you're a radiologist, you're one of many. If you obtain extra training as an interventional radiologist or a neuroradiologist, then you have an additional feather in your cap when it comes to joining a hospital staff or a group practice. Another example comes from the field of psychiatry. If you do a fellowship in child psychiatry, you expand your opportunities—you can specialize in children or broaden and see both adults and children. Simply put, it broadens your possibilities.

In order to obtain a fellowship, you need to be willing to see patients, work with residents, and conduct research. (These will be busy years!) In addition, you may want to indicate that you are planning to become board certified during this time. Program directors will be impressed by your drive.

In your interviews for fellowships, you should be prepared to have some preliminary discussions about your area of research. Think through all the things that interested you in medical school and during your residency but that you didn't have time to explore, and this ought to give you a topic or two to discuss. After that, you will likely get plenty of feedback, and you can refine your plans then.

While undertaking a fellowship requires a great deal of work, it can assure you of obtaining a flexibility that can be highly desirable in a changing job market.

The ℞ for Gaining a Residency

- Work hard at perfecting your personal statement.
- Ask for letters of recommendation early and be organized with the materials.
- Do your homework. Prepare for the interview by reading the application packet and becoming knowledgeable about the faculty.
- Show the interviewer that your skills and interests are simpatico with those of the program.
- Be enthusiastic, yet also be conservative in your attire and attitudes.
- Be organized and ask questions that will allow you to see if you would like the program.
- Explore the facilities and talk to other residents. Some people claim that resident satisfaction should be the number one criterion used to accept or decline an offer.
- Consider continuing on for a fellowship.

9

GETTING CONNECTED: ATTENDING PHYSICIAN INTERVIEWS

Now that you have completed many years of medical school, a residency period, and possibly a fellowship, you are finally ready to practice medicine. For most candidates that's very exciting—until they realize that yet another round of interviews await them if they are actually going to get hired for a job.

A logical first job is that of attending physician at a hospital. When you go out on these interviews, it is often assumed, to a certain degree, that you possess the necessary skills and credentials for the position. You've completed medical school and advanced training and passed the necessary examinations. So instead of checking your credentials, the interviewers will be intent on assessing your interpersonal fit with the facility. For that reason, your ability to make each person feel comfortable and respected may be what wins you the position.

While chapter 4 contains most of what you need to know for your interview, here are some additional pointers to help you emerge victorious when interviewing for a position as an attending physician.

THE HOMEWORK CONTINUES

Before you embark on your first "real" job interview, you'll want to do some necessary homework. (You only *thought* you prepared for your last exam.) Though you've begun the task—at least if you've been following the advice in part one—more groundwork needs to be done to help you tailor your efforts to the current task at hand.

Learning as much as you can about the facility is your first step toward acing the interview. A simple phone call to the local chamber of commerce will provide you with some basic information. Normally, the chamber will have pamphlets they can send to you concerning most hospitals. These pamphlets will contain a great deal of information (e.g., whether the facility is a for-profit or a nonprofit hospital or some other type of institution) and should include directions on what to do if you'd like to know more. The hospital may have a public relations department or a special committee that can provide you with additional details.

You must also educate yourself about the medical staff at a given facility, and this information should also be contained in the brochure about the hospital. You should know the specialties of the top physicians. Examine the other doctors' unique skills and ascertain how you will fit in. For example, you may specialize in a certain type of treatment, or perhaps you're expert at working with special types of patients. If the facility seems to be lacking someone with those specialties, then emphasizing what special training you have to offer may swing the job in your direction.

Your information about the doctors can also be helpful as you go through the interview process. If you're aware of what some of them are known for and are able to talk about their accomplishments and skills, they will be complimented. This can work in your favor.

Additionally, you should examine some basic information about the community the hospital serves. There are many differences between working in a private hospital in a small rural town and a hospital in a large metropolitan area. For example, physicians in large cities in particular must have a solid knowledge base regarding the treatment of AIDS and ways of addressing the needs of patients with this illness.

You should also look into the cultural and religious mix of the community. Some communities have a strong ethnic population that has special needs or unique health issues. If you have expertise in dealing with specific populations, this proficiency may win you the job. For example, being able to speak Spanish and having extensive experience addressing Hispanic patients can be a great asset when applying for a medical job in certain parts of the country.

Overall, be aware that each community has different medical needs to be met by health workers. Be aware of how you will fit into this system.

THE INTERVIEW: MANY FACES, MANY QUESTIONS

A hospital is a complex professional and social system. Many disparate people with distinct types of jobs work there, and each person has a unique outlook and can provide a great deal of information to you concerning the hospital.

Your interview for the position of attending physician will likely consist of meetings with many different people from many different fields and departments. Get as complete a view of life at the hospital as possible by talking to many people in diverse departments. (Don't discount the opinions of secretaries or orderlies as you move from department to department; they'll give you a strong feeling about what the work atmosphere is really like.) Being active in the interview process and talking to many people will help ensure that you learn about the hospital and its staff—both physicians and nonphysicians.

The Medical Director

The medical director is often the first person with whom you will talk after your arrival, and he or she will provide you with details of your agenda for the visit.

Part of this first meeting will involve confirming what you have learned during your earlier research. The position of medical director or chief of staff may vary in different settings. For example, some organizations also have an additional officer that serves as the president of the medical staff. However, your meeting with any of these officials will be important.

The medical director will look more carefully at your medical background than other interviewers. In general, he or she will be evaluating the following:

- **Your academic background.** Although the caliber of the school that you attended may be important, don't worry if you didn't graduate from an Ivy League school. Relatively few people attend the top echelon of schools, and many outstanding physicians come from schools with less sterling reputations.
- **Your current academic credentials.** Having publications and/or research experience is a plus, but if you do not have any published credits, it is not a drawback to your career.
- **Your attitude toward "the system."** As an attending physician, you will be an integral component of the hospital and must uphold your obligations. One area of particular importance to medical directors (who are responsible for assigning physicians to committees) is your willingness to sit on committees and shoulder committee responsibilities. Although this is usually not the most thrilling aspect of a doctor's day, emphasize that you understand the importance of committees and are looking forward to becoming involved. If you have previously chaired or sat on any kind of committee, this should be reflected on your résumé. During the interview, you can also discuss a positive aspect of the experience or something that you learned.
- **Your tolerance for and compliance with paperwork.** Another issue that is of interest to medical directors is that of medical records. With the advent of increased third-party payers, managed care, and quality assurance departments at most hospitals, medical records have also increased in importance. Basically, you will be expected to document every interaction you have with patients. Discuss your experiences with filling out medical records, and don't complain. Though you may acknowledge that the work is not your favorite, show that you are well aware that good documentation can save you and the organization a lot of hassles, including major ones such as lawsuits.

During your meeting with the medical director, you may want to ask about the other physicians. Obtain information concerning who the doctors are, and how many of them are board certified. Ask the medical director about any other VIPs (e.g., people in the community, administration, physicians, or other staff) about whom you should be aware. Solicit information regarding the principal concerns and joys experienced by other physicians at the site. You might also ask whether most of the doctors get along well.

The Administrators

An administrator will not be the primary person checking out your medical competency; the administrator is looking for candidates who have the ability to relate well with patients and others and keep patients happy. This is because the administrator's responsibilities primarily involve handling complaints lodged about doctors from staff and patients. They want to try to avoid lawsuits, and are therefore trying to hire a doctor that will get along with everybody.

For you, this interview is one of your best opportunities to gather some general information. Ask about the philosophy of the hospital and (tactfully) its financial stability, and inquire about the administrator's vision for the future of the facility. You'll also learn a lot if you ask about some of the problems the medical staff committee encounters and what solutions have been developed for overcoming these obstacles.

Keep in mind that administrators have a profound effect on the day-to-day operation of a facility. If you find that you do not like the administrators or their attitudes concerning the facility, you may choose to turn the job down if it is offered.

The Physicians and Other Professionals

When you meet with other physicians and members of the hospital staff (nurses, medical records people, etc.) in other disciplines, try to be as warm and genuine as possible. Treat everyone you talk to with respect. Unfortunately, some physicians can be quite arrogant, particularly with support staff, and this ungiving attitude will backfire when you're trying to get a job. If you come from a well-known school, you'll need to be particularly careful. People may anticipate that you will be arrogant or pompous. A good environment consists of a team of people, all of whom are very good at what they do. Imagine to yourself that all the people you meet at the facility are future colleagues who will help to build the strongest team possible.

KEEP IT A TWO-WAY STREET

In every interview, be sure to ask questions. You'll need this information when it comes time to decide whether or not to accept a position, and it will also make you seem interested and enthusiastic.

While the following list of questions will get you started, take time to sit down before your interview and determine the qualities that you are searching for in a position. You can then devise questions that will best elicit the information you desire.

1. What do you think are the strengths of this facility?
2. What do you think are its weaknesses?
3. What attracted you here and what has prompted you to stay?
4. How do the other attending physicians get along with their colleagues?
5. What resources are available to physicians?

IN THE END, IT'S THE PATIENTS

During your interview, you may talk about or be asked about patient care. Perhaps the fundamental characteristic that doctors must have is respect for patients. If you talk negatively about them, even in a joking manner, you may be immediately disqualified. If you convey your sincere interest in making people feel better, this will be one of the strongest qualifications you can place in your favor.

THE ℞ FOR SUCCESSFUL "ATTENDING"

- Prepare for your interview by acquainting yourself with the staff members and their interests, as well as the orientation of the facility.
- Medical directors will examine your medical knowledge and your attitudes toward medical records and committee attendance.

- Administrators will evaluate your interpersonal skills, as opposed to your knowledge concerning medicine.
- Treat everyone you meet with respect.
- Ask questions so that you'll come away with a better understanding of the facility.
- Don't be negative, particularly when discussing patients.

10

PRACTICING IN ALL THE RIGHT PLACES: INTERVIEWING FOR A GROUP PRACTICE

Working as a part of a group practice used to be the norm, and it's still a common way to practice medicine. What's happening, however, is that the nature of the group practice is changing. Few can continue to exist as fee-for-service operations. Most group practices are picking up affiliations with one or more managed care operations, and the necessity of these connections is changing the nature of the group practice. Physicians must become more conscious of the financial costs of the procedures or tests they are ordering, and the group practice itself must become adept at more effective management of patients in a shorter period of time.

That said, many young doctors will still be joining group practices, and here's what you need to know in order to interview successfully in this type of situation.

THE NATURE OF THE BEAST: UNDERSTANDING TYPES OF PRACTICES

Group practices today can be found in several forms:

Traditional group practice. A group of physicians with the same specialty work together and share their practice. It might be a group of oncologists, dermatologists, or nephrologists. As a group they share an office and an office staff, and cover for each other during weekends or vacations. Typically, funds are split, too. All fees are collected, the income is pooled, and the profits are distributed equally after all expenses are paid.

Multiple specialty clinic. Sometimes "solo practice" doctors will group together to create a practice that shares office space and some staffing. For instance, a physician might join a multidisciplinary group of doctors (internal medicine, psychiatry, radiology, urology, surgery, pediatrics, obstetrics-gynecology, dermatology, etc.) For a group like this, the motivation to add a new member is to fill a specialty gap; they may be lacking a urologist and want to have a very strong person in place for referrals. However, because liability and income are different from specialty to specialty, these practices may be group in appearance but are generally solo in the way the businesses are structured. The system does offer the benefit of sharing some costs, and it definitely increases the likelihood of in-office referrals. If a patient is already comfortable in that environment, he or she is more likely to come back to another specialist within the group.

Hospital practice. A hospital practice may consist of both inpatient and outpatient work. This was a very common type of practice in the past before managed care came into the picture, and still might be the only type of practice in a very small community. In this type of situation, income may be collected by either the hospital or the physician, but in either case, the hospital receives a percentage of all fees.

GROUP PRACTICES ARE STRENGTHENING AFFILIATIONS

You are entering the medical field at a time when great changes are taking place, and if you aspire to enter a group practice, you'll have a first-row seat for much of what is happening.

To build and maintain a healthy customer base, most group practices are affiliating with health maintenance organizations, managed care operations, and/or hospitals in order to be where the patients are. (As you're undoubtedly aware, numerous employers have changed their insurance plans, with the result that many patients have had to leave long relationships with their doctors in order to get coverage through their employer's group plans.) The benefits of affiliating involve marketing and holding on to customers/patients. The drawbacks, depending on the operation with which the practice affiliates and the details of the contract, can involve extra paperwork and meeting certain administrative requirements in running the office.

When interviewing, you would certainly want to ask the various people you meet how they feel about the affiliation. Their comments, both positive and negative, will give you insight as to what your day-to-day work life would be if you were to take a job there. (Would you be sweating over paperwork? Rushing to fit in a certain number of patients?)

QUALITY COUNTS IN QUALIFYING FOR A GROUP PRACTICE

When you interview for a position in a group practice, you may meet with the partners individually, or you may meet with two or three of them at a time. To some extent, they are looking for a certain expertise. For instance, if there are already six to eight general radiologists in the group and you are the only neuroradiologist or interventional radiologist, then your particular specialty is likely something they will consider an asset to the practice.

While a group is always happy to bring in someone with an impressive list of credentials and published articles, the most important qualities involve helping the group function well as a team. For that reason, one of the most important qualities they look for is a willingness to work hard. (Because many group practices operate through equal distribution of profits, nobody wants to bring another person into the group who works less hard but gets paid equally.) Describing to your interviewers personal anecdotes that stress your willingness to work hard can stand you in good stead.

An ability to get along with others, including other doctors, nurses, and the office staff, is also a strong asset to any practice. Who wants to work with a prima donna, a troublemaker, or a complainer?

Flexibility is also a key. There may be schedule changes and work or personal life disruptions, and a good group physician needs to be able to take all of this in stride.

In a group practice, the interviewers will be intimately involved with a new partner, including years of working closely, covering for each other when on call, and almost surely sharing financial resources. They don't want to hire someone and then feel stuck with him or her, so group members take the interview process very seriously. The process may be a slow one, so that each member can meet and spend time with you, and they will be watching every aspect of your behavior.

Sometimes a group will invite a potential new hire to work alongside them for one to three weeks (with reasonable compensation) just to see how well that person fits in. (To do this, you have to be licensed or will have to obtain a license to practice medicine in the state before participating in such an opportunity.) If this trial period can be worked out, the benefits are many. The group becomes comfortable with the candidate before having to make a firm financial offer, while the candidate gets to know her or his future colleagues better and learns something about the everyday operation of the practice. It also offers some financial help—something that most people need badly when starting out, because the post–medical school bills can be considerable.

Once hired, many group practices do not accept a newcomer as a partner right away, and may ask him or her to work on a salary basis for one to three years before offering a partnership. In reality, this is a smart and perhaps fair way to get know the individual well.

WHAT TO LOOK FOR IN A GOOD GROUP PRACTICE TODAY

As with any job possibility, you need to observe with a critical eye as you go through the interview process. You're considering a position that could last a lifetime, and you want to be sure you're making the right decision.

Because so much change is in the wind in the medical profession, one key element you'll want to see in the group practice you join is a sign that the partners are keenly aware of what's going on and are more than willing to change as they need to in order to remain a viable group practice. Older doctors who "remember when" may be a part of the mix, and if there are enough of them who are resistant to change, this doesn't bode well for your future. In general, consider the following:

- Does the practice have a relationship with an HMO or a managed care plan?
- Does it have a relationship with a hospital?
- Is it affiliated with an academic center, or is it community-based?
- Could it effectively compete for patients as part of an overall health plan?
- How well is it managed, and how efficiently does it operate in comparison with similar groups in the community?
- Does it have effective leadership and a management structure that will allow for prompt decisions?
- What are the career aspirations of the members, and how willing are they to make changes when necessary?
- Do the physicians have good reputations and seem to hold solid values?

Group practices that survive and prosper in the current environment are those with established relations with successful, growing managed care organizations; those that have strong relationships with hospitals that could effectively manage or partner with group practices; those with strong physician leadership; and those freestanding primary care group practices that are well managed.

BEING AN ASSET TO THE GROUP

Once hired, practicing good medicine is just the beginning for a group member who is going to be successful. To help your group weather any future changes, you can do several things:

- Stay informed about health care system reform policy options on both the national and state level.

- Get involved in your local and state medical societies, and consider participating in other industry groups.
- Be prepared for change and be open to new ideas. There are always opportunities for those who are open-minded enough to stay current with what is happening.

The ℞ for Becoming Part of a Group

- Be aware of the different structures of group practices so that you'll understand the nature of the ones to which you're applying.
- A willingness to work hard is perhaps one of the most important qualities to have if you want to join a group practice.
- Candidates who are flexible and have the ability to work well with others will be attractive to members of a group practice.
- As you interview, assess whether the group has its eye on the future. In order to survive, group practices will need to be ready to adapt to what's going on around them.
- Once hired, stay informed about changes in the health care system, and get involved in local and state medical societies so that you'll be abreast with what's happening.

11

SURVIVING THE MANAGED CARE INTERVIEW

Managed care has exploded over the last decade; more than 50 million Americans currently belong to a health maintenance organization (HMO) of some type. This has had a dramatic effect on the practice of medicine, creating an increasing demand for internists or family practitioners who are interested in working as primary care physicians within health maintenance organizations.

When it comes to job-hunting, you may find that health maintenance organizations offer work opportunities for physicians that will provide you with stability of employment along with flexibility of tasks that can be quite intriguing.

THE ABCS OF HMOS AND PPOS

The concept of HMOs can possibly best be dated to the 1970s, when the government was seeking a sensible way to bring "preventive medicine to the masses." Managed care was an attempt to control consumer health care spending while providing all-encompassing medical services for a fixed fee to every person who joined the HMO, regardless of the amount of per person use.

Preferred provider organization (PPOs) are similar to HMOs. Consumers must utilize the services of physicians who are designated providers for their plan in order to receive full benefits. If they use other physicians without a referral from their preferred provider, then it costs the consumer more money. These systems stand in contrast to the pay-for-services model in which the insurance company (or the patient) pays a physician for whatever services are provided to the patient during a particular office visit.

The key feature of HMOs and PPOs is the concept of the primary health care physician acting as gatekeeper. This primary care physician controls access to most services and is relied on to ensure appropriate utilization of those services.

What this has meant to the medical profession is a shift in the types of jobs that are available and, to some extent, some shifts in the type of work that a primary physician performs. Because of the need for gatekeepers, there has been an increase in the need for pediatricians and family practitioners, while there has been a decrease in the need for some types of specialists. (There are exceptions, however. One allergist connected with an HMO says he's busier than ever now because through the HMO people can afford to come to him. When he worked only on a fee-for-services basis, the allergist was a luxury many consumers couldn't afford.)

BENEFITS OF AN HMO OR PPO

Physicians who are part of a managed care system report the following benefits:

1. They like providing continuity of care for their patients. As gatekeeper, you are closely involved with your patients when a problem comes along. You can be your patients' case manager and oversee all of their health care in a way that was not possible before.
2. They needn't worry about looking for business because HMOs and PPOs provide marketing for their practice. HMO-sponsored advertising appears in newsletters, public presentations, and publications at no cost to the physician.
3. They build up a nice client base. It is easier in some ways to preserve your client base under an HMO or PPO because patients basically have to apply to change physicians. If they are generally

pleased with you and the care you provide, they are not likely to change to someone unknown.
4. They can maintain a relatively stable income each year.

However, HMOs don't necessarily offer utopia. A managed care program is just that—managed—so you'll want to evaluate whether you feel that this particular organization is one you like. Here are some suggestions on doing well at the interview and picking up on clues as to whether or not this is the HMO for you.

BEFORE THE INTERVIEW: EDUCATE YOURSELF

In order to excel at an interview with a managed care company, you need to understand the system. Although an HMO will not expect you to know everything about their organization, you will probably have a smoother and more impressive interview if you understand the basics.

You can get information from the HMO or PPO regarding the specifics of their organization, and you might consult professional journals for information on managed care in your field. Managed care is different for pediatrics and oncology, for example, and you'll help yourself immensely if you can be educated and informed.

If you need help finding relevant articles, just go to your local university medical library and use MEDLINE (or a similar service) to do a search. (A reference librarian can help you if you've never used MEDLINE before.) This extra effort is relatively simple, but can pay off during the interview by making you seem very well informed.

In general, physicians who do well in HMOs

- stay up-to-date on his or her own field, as well as overlapping fields, in order to offer the best care possible
- are reasonably comfortable treating certain illnesses without a full battery of screening tests and are comfortable with basic laboratory tests that rule in or rule out specific diseases
- are comfortable taking care of patients with all types and severities of illness

- would not feel the need to hospitalize patients for routine procedures (things that could be done on an outpatient basis)
- would feel comfortable enlisting the family's help in caring for a patient rather than hospitalizing a patient

DURING THE INTERVIEW: RESPECT YOUR INTERVIEWERS

When you apply to a managed care company, you will likely be interviewed by a wide variety of people—everyone from the other doctors who work for it to the businesspeople who oversee the management side.

For the most part, the HMO interview will focus on your ability to supply medical services to consumers in an efficient manner. Managed care companies want physicians who can balance patient satisfaction and well-being with efficiency and cost-effectiveness.

Talk about Your Qualifications

Although HMOs are run for profit, people who head these companies also care about the quality of care provided. They want physicians who are very good at what they do, so at the interview you'll want to emphasize that you are

- well trained
- board certified (or signed up to take the boards)
- an excellent diagnostician

Don't be afraid to brag about yourself a little. You will probably not offend the interviewer by explaining that you are a strong candidate and will be an asset to his or her company.

Show That You Can Be a Team Player

In traditional non-managed care systems, the physician, in consultation with the patient, makes all of the health care decisions. In contrast,

HMOs depend upon many people contributing to decisions in order to help ensure that cost-effectiveness is always kept in mind: patients choose their providers; clinical practitioners perform peer reviews; physicians make medical decisions; and all of this must be approved by nonclinical case managers who oversee the implementation and distribution of services.

A managed care physician will need to work with the case managers. You must feel comfortable interacting with people who may or may not be physicians but who have questions regarding how you treat your patients. The case manager may even have suggestions about the patients' care. This situation can be difficult for physicians who are used to making their own decisions, but is quite tolerable for more team-oriented physicians.

Managed care physicians also must be comfortable asking for consultations or second opinions from other professionals without necessarily having to send the patient on to see the specialist right away.

Overall, it is crucial to the managed care company that you work well with others within the group. HMOs do not want to hire physicians who will be difficult, demanding, or hard to work with.

Talk About Your Flexibility

Working hours for HMOs vary from company to company; for the most part, however, flexibility is very important. If you are a patient's preferred provider, you need to be available, or on call, at all times to make decisions regarding their care. However, you will also have other doctors within the group who are capable of covering for you for all but major issues, so your days off can sometimes be worry free. Some large organizations even use nurse practitioners to screen telephone calls, meaning that the only off-hours calls you would need to take from patients would be those of a serious nature. Minor issues would be dealt with by the staff of nurse practitioners.

Since managed care programs generally work with a prescribed formulary and want their physicians to prescribe based on this approved list of medications, you may also want to emphasize that you will adapt to prescribing from the company's formulary list. Get a copy of the formulary ahead of time and familiarize yourself with what is and is not on it. If one of your preferred medications is missing, bone up on the replacement. You may even want to get some articles from professional journals about the replacement. This extra effort will also help you decide whether you can live with the company's formulary. (If you can't, then this isn't the employer for you.)

DOING YOUR HOMEWORK FOR YOUR OWN DECISION MAKING

Because a managed care operation comes with a certain set of parameters, it is particularly important that you do enough homework on the company to know that their procedures are ones with which you are comfortable. Paying attention to everything—from their formulary to their preferred methods for specialist referral—is vital to making sure that this is a company with which you'll be a fit. As you research:

- Look at how much and what kind of paperwork will be necessary.
- Listen to how the case managers oversee patient management. (Some companies have a vigorous level of supervision, and you need to be prepared for that.)
- Ask about performance reviews and on what criteria your performance is reviewed.
- Find out about what support you'll have available (nurse practitioners, physicians' assistants, etc.).
- Ask about policy on referring patients to other doctors. Some organizations have financial penalties for too many referrals to specialists, and this may not be something with which you are comfortable.

Compare the various places you apply to on every factor that is important to you. After all, you probably don't want to work for a company that has policies with which you openly disagree.

The ℞ for HMO Happiness

- The benefits of working for an HMO include providing continuity of care for your patients and not having to worry about marketing your practice. However, you have to be prepared to work within the managed care system, and have someone supervising the care you provide.
- To interview well, learn all you can about the managed care system and the specifics about the company with whom you are interviewing.
- Managed care companies need skilled diagnosticians. Don't be afraid to emphasize your medical skills and abilities.
- Discuss your willingness to be a team player, since patient care will involve more than just your own input.
- Look into the company formulary to be certain it's one with which you are comfortable.
- Learn as much as you can about the company before you accept a job. Know how much paperwork is required, be certain you like the staff with whom you'll work, and talk about their policy on patient referrals. Before signing on, you want to make certain this job is a fit for you.

12

"SO YOU WANT TO TEACH?" FACULTY POSITION INTERVIEWS

Applying to become a faculty member at a medical school brings with it both good news and bad news. The bad news is that it requires a great deal of preparation, as candidates are almost always expected to conduct a colloquium where their research is presented and discussed. However, the good news is that you are no longer a student and have risen above student status. If you are a strong candidate, you may even be courted for the job, making the interview a pleasant and exciting experience.

Unfortunately, the competition for jobs in academia is tough. All positions receive far more applicants than openings; ratios of a hundred applications for one position are not unusual! What's more, after the interview process, medical centers sometimes decide not to hire any applicants, if they are not satisfied with the applicant pool. You must obviously be very well prepared for this interview in order to succeed.

Unlike the interviews you may have encountered when you applied to medical school, when applying for a faculty position, you will not simply be answering questions during a designated interview session with one or two interviewers. Instead, the process will last one or two days; you will meet with many people, and you will have to be generally much more active during the whole process.

The process itself generally consists of three identifiable parts:

1. the screening process
2. the formal interview
3. the colloquium

This chapter includes discussions of each of these components to help you prepare and organize yourself for the interview.

WHO'S IN, WHO'S OUT: THE SCREENING PROCESS

The initial screening of candidates generally consists of examining each person's curriculum vitae (c.v.) and related materials to select only the most qualified for the more time-consuming and rigorous interview process.

The medical center will be considering your education, the medical school from which you graduated, and where and when you did your residency and fellowship. They will also examine your c.v., any materials you've had published, and will take into account other experiences that might make you particularly well qualified for their facility. For example, if the center is increasing its gastrointestinal services and you are a radiologist with an expertise in working with patients with liver problems, then the department of radiology might consider you a real find because your expertise will be valuable for the facility's long-term plans.

For this reason, it is vital that you prepare for submission an excellent package of materials. Look back at chapter 3 and take time to prepare a thoughtful, concise cover letter. It should clearly state why you are well suited for the job. Before sending it, be certain that you have properly spelled the name of the person to whom the material is to be sent and that your cover letter has no errors. Also make certain that your c.v. is up to date and that the copies of any published materials are highly readable photocopies.

Typically, only three to five candidates are selected for a formal interview, so it is a particularly favorable sign that you are a strong candidate if you receive an interview.

UP CLOSE AND PERSONAL: THE FORMAL INTERVIEW

The formal interview is the next step in your quest for a faculty position. Rather than being a single interview, it's really a series of interviews. You will generally be expected to visit the facility for at least a day—often two. Most of the time will be fully scheduled with meeting various people (and being interviewed) and being shown various parts of the medical center and school. Sometimes candidates are so tightly booked they find that one of the most stressful aspects of the process is trying to be on time for each of the many appointments, particularly since discussions and tours frequently run over the allotted time.

Expect to be interviewed by virtually every faculty member in your department as well as some "significant others" from other parts of the school (including the dean of the school of medicine for some positions). Some of these interviews may be formal, but others will not be. You may have breakfast with one or more faculty members, while another gives you a tour. Although these situations may not seem like interviews, remember that you are always being evaluated.

As with any interview, expect to be asked many tough questions. Be straightforward and genuine in your answers while stressing your ability to be a good colleague. Some common questions you may be asked include:

1. Describe your specialty training.
2. What research have you recently undertaken?
3. How do you foresee developing your research interests if you were here?
4. How would you describe yourself as an instructor?
5. How do you feel about advising medical students?
6. What resources (e.g., medical equipment, personnel) do you foresee needing to conduct your research?
7. What are the subjects you'd like to teach?
8. How will you meet the needs of the department?
9. How many days per week are you willing to invest in being in the clinic or visiting the ward? (How many patients are you willing to oversee?)

In addition to meeting with many faculty members, you may be requested to meet with chief residents or other trainees. Although you may be tempted to relax during this interview, it is important to make a favorable impression with the students also. Though the trainees may not have a vote in personnel decisions, their general input is usually requested. Positive or negative feedback may have great impact. (It's always important to treat everyone you encounter with high regard.)

Name-Dropping: Go Easy
One mistake faculty candidates sometimes make is to refer too often to their adviser from medical school, particularly if this person is well known. Given that you may have worked with him or her for many years, this overemphasis is understandable, but it doesn't explain much about your qualities, and it can put off interviewers. They want you to recognize the virtues and strengths of their staff and facility.

Riding someone else's coattails is a ride to nowhere when it comes to job interviewing.

COMPETENCE WITH A CAPITAL "C"

Competence is the most important characteristic to display at an interview for a faculty position. As a future faculty member, you will be dealing with colleagues and students and must display that you know a great deal about your area of expertise.

The academic journal *Organizational Behavior and Human Decision Process* published the results of a study in which potential job applicants were rated in terms of perceived competence. In general, applicants with higher perceived competence received higher ratings of suitability for the position. This finding may not be surprising, but it highlights the importance of this trait.

You can help convey competence by highlighting your:

Credentials. Departments will look for applicants with publications and a history of being able to secure grants. These elements of your credentials should be reflected in your vita. However, don't be shy about discussing publications and grants during your interview.

Credibility. Competence can also be displayed by talking with authority about your research, displaying a sense of humor, and showing that you can work and have fun with others. Being able to add a touch of lightness to your interviews and colloquium is an expression of security; anyone who is overwrought with nervousness takes on an overly serious demeanor.

Confidence. The confidently delivered colloquium that is presented with authority will be a strong asset if you are to be favored with a job offer.

THE COLLOQUIUM

During the formal interview period, you will most likely be asked to conduct a colloquium on your area of expertise. Some people assert that the colloquium is the most important aspect of your interview, so you'll want to be thoroughly prepared.

Your topic for your colloquium should relate to the position for which you're applying. Sometimes applicants need to reslant their research material, depending on where they're applying. Faculty members can be very competitive and may not want new hires to have an area of focus that is too close to their own. For this reason, take into account the special emphasis of faculty members in your field at a particular facility and attempt to distinguish yourself in a noncompetitive way. For example, if you do research in endocrinology and several other faculty members do as well, emphasize your particular expertise and type of training and how it will fit in with the department. Remember that most departments strive to have an array of different types of instructors and researchers, so they'll want to know how your background will enrich what they are already doing.

Depending on the facility where you're presenting, you may be expected to speak anywhere from 1 to 1.5 hours (with questions and discussion). Call ahead and ask what the estimated presentation time will be, but still be prepared to cope with the unexpected. The committee may ultimately have less (or more) time for your presentation than they had anticipated, so your talk should be put together in such a way that you can add or subtract from it as necessary.

It is imperative that your lecture be well prepared and smoothly presented. Your presentation style should be straightforward, conversational, and not dry. You don't want to lecture. Follow your notes so that you don't make mistakes, but don't simply read from them. You should know the colloquium well enough that you can present it in your own words, using your notes only as an outline. Too often, medical school faculty applicants will talk in citations, and make their presentations dense and overly technical. Deliver your presentation in a friendly and interesting manner, and involve your audience by posing questions or dilemmas or citing mysteries that interested you as you pursued your research. Carefully rehearsed jokes can also liven things up.

Slides and other graphic presentations are strongly recommended as they can enhance a talk and give people something to look at during your presentation. (An appropriate cartoon shown during your slide presentation can be a fun idea.) However, practice using these methods so that you are not nervous about them or that minor mistakes such as a jammed slide will not unduly fluster you.

If possible, practice presenting your colloquium to an audience; perhaps you can arrange to speak at a small conference or to a group of your peers before your interview.

During your colloquium, make sure that you adequately answer all questions that are posed to you. Listen with care to audience comments so that you can answer everyone's questions, and even an irrelevant question should be treated as a good question.

Be prepared to answer detailed and specific questions concerning the research design method, statistical procedures, subject sampling method, and other relevant details. Remember that each faculty member will have a particular bias based upon his or her interests and may ask questions that they find relevant to his or her own work. In order to have a successful overall interview, you must answer these questions well enough to satisfy each faculty member.

Most faculty members will not try to trip you up with difficult questions, so take your time with any question that catches you off guard. If you ask for clarification from the questioner, you will likely find that he or she is more than willing to explain the nature of the question, treating you like a potential colleague.

If you do not know the answer to one of the questions, be honest. Say that you're not sure of this answer and would appreciate it if the audience has any information about this particular topic. This may stimulate discussion.

Presenting successfully at your colloquium will be a definite feather in your cap. If it goes less well than you would have hoped, view it as a learning experience, and make some notes about what you need to work on before the next time.

FINDING OUT WHAT YOU NEED TO KNOW

As with most interviews, this is also the time for *you* to interview the employer and decide if you could be happy at this medical center.

Typically, you will be given a thorough tour of the medical center and general campus. Ask many question, about the facilities and its resources. After all, you may spend many years, if not your entire career, at the medical center if you accept an offer.

Try to determine if the university and surrounding area will offer the needed resources for you to conduct your research (lab space, specific medical populations for research, personnel).

You must remember there will be a great deal of expectation placed upon you. In order to obtain tenure at most universities, you must publish articles, and you'll need to have the available resources to conduct your research. It will not do you much good to accept a job if you will not be able to fulfill the requirements to keep it (and earn tenure).

Also, carefully assess the surrounding city or town to evaluate whether or not the lifestyle would be to your liking. Look carefully at the community. Does it have the type of shopping places, restaurants, or leisure activities that can help you be happy there? If not, is there a town nearby that would fulfill some of what is missing?

Some applicants may be desperate and accept a job that's not really right for them. Try to do your homework and to keep your options open so that you needn't settle for a location where you'll be unhappy. With luck, the job you accept now will be one where you can stay for a long time.

WHAT YOU NEED TO KNOW ABOUT A TEACHING JOB

While any sort of financial or job-related negotiation would only take place after you received a job offer, you still need to find out some specifics and may want to ask questions such as the following:

1. What yearly income is being offered with the position?
2. What start-up costs (moving costs, computer money, lab funds) are offered?
3. What lab space is available?
4. What office space is available?
5. How much merit money is available, especially for newer faculty?
6. What are the teaching expectations?

Before you accept an offer, be sure that all of these questions have been answered to your satisfaction.

Tenure

Ask about tenure when you are investigating each facility. If you receive and accept a job offer, you will have to begin working for tenure immediately, so it is helpful to understand the system ahead of time. At some facilities, receiving tenure is much more difficult (if not impossible) than at other places.

It's helpful to talk to some recently tenured faculty. As you are introduced around, you will almost certainly meet some of these people (or you can telephone them afterward if it seems as though a job offer is a likely possibility). Some questions that will be helpful are the following:

1. How many publication credits did you have when you got tenure?
2. Did the tenure process go smoothly?
3. How many people have been denied tenure while you've been here?
4. Did the facility supply you with the resources you needed to get tenure?
5. Would you take this job again if you had a choice?

> If you find that the burdens at a particular facility are too overwhelming, it may help you decide to continue your job search or take another offer. If the atmosphere is unpleasant in the long run, it will be difficult to be happy.

EXPENSES

Normally the medical center will pay for your costs, such as airplane ticket and a hotel room. However, this may not always be the case, so be prepared to pay for some costs, particularly for meals. (Refer to chapter 2 for more information on handling expenses for any job interview.)

The "Faculty"

As you go through the faculty interview process, keep the following in mind:

- The first screening of applicants is done by sifting through c.v.'s and related materials. Be certain your "paper" package (the written material explaining your qualifications) is an excellent one.
- You will likely spend at least one day (and maybe two) at the facility, so be prepared for a marathon of interviews.
- Prepare thoroughly for your colloquium. Your presentation must be professional and approachable for the faculty members.
- Keep asking questions throughout your visit. If they should offer you the position, you'll want to have learned enough about the community to feel that you'll be happy there.
- Find out about tenure. Sometimes the pressure to qualify for tenure can be very high, and you may not want to live that way for the next few years.
- Negotiate carefully before you accept a position.

13

GO TO THE HEAD OF THE CLASS: DIRECTORSHIP INTERVIEWS

One of the most important types of interviews is the medical directorship (also referred to as the chief of staff) interview. During it, there are many expectations you should fulfill because you must embody the future vision of the facility. The direction that the facility takes will be dependent upon you. Thus, *the interviewer will want to make absolutely sure that you are unequivocally the best applicant for the job.*

(While this chapter is written to help people who are applying for medical directorships, the advice contained within is also appropriate for those aspiring to be a department chair or even the dean of school of medicine.)

Hiring a top medical executive is a tremendous investment for the organization. Not only do they have to pay a sizable salary, many costs are associated with hiring a new director and much time is required while a new person settles into the job and begins to function at full capacity. Employers who are hiring a director want to make sure that the person they hire will be able to perform the job in a superior manner. Because the interviewer is looking for Mr. or Ms. Perfect, he or she will scrutinize your qualifications carefully and may want to obtain information about nonprofessional aspects of your life such as your family, religion, and culture. Almost any topic will be fair game. Rising to this level of professionalism and triumphing during such an interview can be a tremendous challenge.

Normally you will be interviewed by other high-ranking health care professionals. Remember that the people who interview you are the top people in the organization, and you need to show them respect and listen carefully to everything they have to say. However, the interviewers will also want evidence of your leadership skills. Thus you cannot defer to the interviewers' authority too much. Quite a balancing act!

In this chapter we will outline some of the things you should consider before you are interviewed for a medical directorship. You need to present yourself to the best of your ability while maintaining a delicate balance between your display of respect and assertiveness.

LINING UP THE INTERVIEW: THE COVER LETTER

For most directorship interviews, your first approach—whether you're answering an ad or submitting your curriculum vitae because you were recommended for the job—will be in writing, and this will be your first chance to explain how well-suited you are for the job. For this reason, it is important that your c.v. (see Appendix A) and your cover letter be well planned. This is your chance to highlight how your experience matches the job for which you are applying. For example, your contact may have mentioned that three years' experience managing health care employees is required, and your cover letter can emphasize your experience in this area.

Martin Yate's "executive briefing," described in chapter 3, is perfect for this approach. It allows a potential employer to quickly scan your credentials to determine if you should be interviewed. The process indicates that you carefully considered the job requirements before you decided to apply. It also indicates that you are thoughtful, conscientious, and well organized.

With luck, you'll soon be among the applicants whom they call for an interview.

FAMILIARIZE YOURSELF WITH THE FACILITY

Because of the magnitude of the job, it is vital that you do your homework prior to the interview. The likelihood of your getting the job will be greatly increased if you show a working knowledge of the facility and some of the issues they may be facing.

Find out in detail what kind of patients the facility serves. If you don't live locally, try consulting the Better Business Bureau or the local chamber of commerce for this kind of information; or, if you know local doctors or nurses, they will be able to provide you with helpful information. The brochures the organization sends out will also provide information on their areas of strength. In addition, find out what the facility's area of specialty is. In what departments does it take the most pride?

You should also make yourself aware of the facility's competition. What other hospitals in the area provide similar services? What services does the facility offer and how do they differ from those of the competition? Which facilities are doing well in this area and which are not doing well? (The answers to these questions may also influence how hard you fight for the job. If you're impressed by one of the competing facilities, you may want to apply there, too.) You may find that a particular facility provides exactly the kind of services that you prefer, and that will be a very positive discussion point for your interview.

Also try to do a little research on the person with whom you'll have your interview. For example, if you read in the newspaper (or learned from a friend) that your interviewer, Dr. Dunlop, recently helped to devise a new surgical technique, you can congratulate him. (To find out a little more about your interviewer, talk to colleagues of his if you know any, or chat for a few minutes with the secretary or administrative assistant who is arranging your interview. A person who works in this position is definitely knowledgeable, and if you explain that you'd like to know a little more about his or her boss in preparation for your interview, chances are he or she will be happy to help you out.) Doing so will make Dr. Dunlop feel good and lets him know that you are knowledgeable about the facility and the health care profession.

PRESENTING YOURSELF WELL

Before the interview, sit down and list your responsibilities in previous positions and try to think about some of the valuable skills you obtained during this employment, particularly as they apply to what you've learned about the facility.

Many employers think that the best predictor of future success in a position is past success, and they will ask many questions about your past performance. Indeed, many interviews focus so much on past behavior that they are called behavior-based interviews.

If you are currently unemployed or no longer working as a medical director, one question that merits special attention is, "Why did you leave your last job?" We recommend you be straightforward. However, some answers are obviously more acceptable than others. For example, do not respond that you left because you were forced to or because your boss was an idiot. Instead, focus on your desire to move ahead and excel with another facility. Perhaps you had advanced as far as you could in your last job and wanted to seek new employment. In this case, stress that you perceive the facility for which you are currently interviewing as having a great deal of potential and you find that exciting. *Never say anything negative about a past job. Instead, present it as a learning experience that helped you develop your skills.*

QUESTIONS TO ASK

The interview is the time for you to exhibit interest in working for the facility. However, bear in mind that the quality of the questions you ask is being judged by the interviewer. Asking naive questions can lead to the assumption that you are unqualified for the job and do not have enough experience. In contrast, if you are able to ask intelligent and informed questions, the interviewer will assume that you are well qualified for the job.

Employers want a medical director who will not require much initial training or supervision. Asking intelligent questions will help show that you are fully prepared to take on the position. Sample questions include:

1. What is the current vision or direction of the facility?
2. What are your expectations for this position?
3. What are the major challenges to be undertaken within the next year?
4. Who has contributed most to the facility recently, and in what way?
5. What have been the recent trends in revenues and expenses for the facility?
6. What relationship have past directors had with the physicians and other employees at this facility?

MANY FACES: THE PANEL INTERVIEW

Many facilities conduct panel interviews during their search for a medical director. During this interview, a group of interviewers—usually 5 to 10 physicians and hospital administrators—question you collectively. This type of interview saves time for the facility, as the key players in the organization can be present at one time. In addition, the interviewers can all see and hear your responses jointly. Thus, they have much about you to discuss after you leave.

The panel interview is also another way that the interviewers can see how you handle pressure. Obviously, being interrogated by several people can induce a great deal of stress, even for the very calm. If you have a hard time staying calm during these times, refer to chapter 16 ("Avoiding the Sweaty Palms Syndrome: Managing Your Anxiety") for a discussion of coping methods for dealing with excessive stress.

The key to the panel interview is to stay as calm and unruffled as possible. Listen carefully to everyone who is talking and make sure not to interrupt anyone. Sometimes one or more of the interviewers may intentionally or inadvertently give you a hard time. Remember that the interviewers may try to show off to the other interviewers by asking overly intellectual questions or attacking your views. In this case, do not allow your temper to show and do not get flustered. The best way to deal with this situation is to use humor or smile to show that you did not take the attack personally. See chapter 5 for additional guidance regarding panel interviews.

TAKE CHARGE AND INTERVIEW ACTIVELY

Interviewing for a top position is different from other job interviews where applicants normally should let the interviewer control the situation. In this case, interviewers want an applicant who displays the ability to be a leader, not someone who is passive or weak. Medical directors will need to deal with everything from physicians who aren't pulling their weight at a facility to problems that arise with the hospital or facility board, so it is vital to convey that you can command difficult situations. As a result, you're going to want to display strength of character and an appropriate degree of assertiveness. Being assertive also exhibits your confidence, which is an important quality you'll need if you get the job. As a director, you will be one of the most significant representatives of the facility. You will set the tone during meetings with employees or patients.

Overall, make sure the interview does not fall into a predictable pattern of the interviewer asking you a question and then you asking a question. Develop a dialog between the two of you. Rapport will be enhanced and the interview will flow more smoothly. In addition, you will be more likely to be able to discuss issues that are important to you. Remember that the interviewer wants someone with strong leadership qualities, so you don't want to be passive during the interview.

How to be assertive without being overbearing? In addition to your general demeanor, you'll have the opportunity to exhibit an authoritative approach when answering questions.

State your position in a composed and firm manner. Don't appear hesitant to give your views. Of course, you should recognize the difference between being assertive and being aggressive. Don't be rude to the interviewer or step on his toes. *Interviewers do not want to feel that you will be a threat to them if you are hired. No matter how loyal an employee may be to the facility, that employee will also want to protect his position.*

Additional methods of displaying assertiveness during your interview include taking appropriate credit for positive events, championing your achievements, and ingratiating yourself with the interviewer without acting obsequious.

Be assertive and don't be afraid to show your toughness, not via an angry interaction but in a calm, problem-solving manner. If you are presented with a hypothetical situation and are asked to describe your course of action, you should be able to consider the various available alternatives. For example, if the interviewer asks how you would handle a physician who was not upholding his responsibilities by keeping adequate medical records, you could state that you might begin by talking to the employee and would not reprimand him unless the dilemma persisted, and that under no circumstances would you embarrass him in front of other employees.

AN EXPERT IN YOUR FIELD

An important trait that interviewers are looking for in a medical director is knowledgeability about the field of medicine. Be aware of the trends and policies of the Joint Commission of Accreditation of Hospital Organizations (JCAHO) and in your field, and you should be particularly comfortable discussing your area of specialization. Additionally, you should understand the structure of the managed care system (also refer to chapter 11, "Surviving the Managed Care Interview"). Likewise, you should know the roles of other professionals working in a hospital setting. Overall, medical directors must be on the cutting edge of their field and have an exceptional knowledge base.

In addition to knowing about medicine, most medical directors today have a working knowledge of computers, not only of functions such as e-mail and word processing, but also the basics about some of the different computer programs used by medical staffs today. After all, being a medical director combines science and medicine with the business world, and you must understand each. Doing this may entail having some conceptual knowledge about technology.

If you don't already possess this knowledge, spend some time educating yourself. You needn't try to speak technobabble during your interview (something that's actually very distracting), but it is knowledge that is important to have.

ORGANIZATION IS KEY

As an executive, it will be your responsibility to organize physicians, employees, patients, and resources. To show that you can organize people and resources, you must first show that *you* are organized. Come into the interview thoroughly prepared. Obviously you must be on time. Your briefcase and any papers you are carrying should be neat and well organized. Have a pad of paper easily accessible to begin taking notes.

Another way to show that you have this skill is to give specific examples of when you have had to organize people or things in the past. Describe in detail how many people you were in charge of in your previous position(s) and tell how you were able to organize everything. If you do not have a great deal of experience in this area, talk about something that you have had to organize that was successful. For example, maybe in your last job you were the chairman of infection control, or pharmacy and therapeutics. These tasks require adeptness at organization, and that's important.

DEMONSTRATE YOUR ABILITY TO DELEGATE

Another key task of a medical director is the delegation of responsibilities. As director, you will be in charge of many different areas, including the management of employees, the overall functioning of committees, and the training of residents or interns. Though you are not necessarily directly involved in all that you oversee, you are responsible for making sure that these tasks are being done correctly.

Completing tasks yourself may be the best way to make sure that they are done properly, but you will have far too many responsibilities (some more important than others) to do them all yourself. For that reason, you have to decide which tasks you will do personally, which tasks will be better taken care of by other employees, and which employee can best carry out each task.

Think of examples of times when you had to delegate responsibilities. If you already have any experience as a director, this chore should be easy. Give as much detail as possible during the interview. In addition, talk about the outcome of your actions. For example, a physician to whom you delegated a responsibility may have displayed an unusual talent for that task. Describe why you chose that employee for the task and why the match worked so well.

You might also talk about an example of a time you delegated responsibility to an employee and it did not work well. For example, the employee may have been too inexperienced for the task or may have not taken the responsibility seriously. In this case, discuss the fact that you recognized the problem and took immediate steps to fix it. Discussing decisions that did not work out well can be fine as long as you stress the methods you used to correct the problem as well.

DEVOTED TO YOUR WORK? YOU NEED TO SAY SO

Medical directors may work 60 to 80 hours or more a week, staying late each night until the work is finished. In addition, many medical directors work seven days a week to help oversee the day-to-day workings of the facility. As the medical head of a facility, you must be willing to work harder than anyone else. It is imperative that you give 100 percent to your job, and this is an important point to convey in the interview.

These long hours may include working late and going on trips or attending conferences, which may prevent you from spending much time with your family. If you have a spouse or family, stress to the interviewer the ways in which you have been able to cope with working long hours in the past and still maintain a happy family life. For example, you can discuss the fact that for the last twelve years you've had excellent household help, and this has permitted both your spouse and yourself to have demanding careers while still feeling the family is well cared for. Discuss how this arrangement has made it easier for you to work such long hours and still be happy.

SHOW THAT YOU HAVE VISION

A medical director must have clear ideas about the direction in which she or he wants to take the facility. Now that you have studied the facility and know a great deal about what it does, try to think of what you might do to make it stronger. What are the facility's weaknesses and how might they realistically be resolved? What are the facility's strengths and how might you build upon these? Demonstrate innovation in your ideas, but be practical as well.

Organize these ideas and simulate preparation for a hospital board meeting. During most interviews, you will be asked to expound upon any ideas that you have for the facility. If you are able to present inventive, informed, and cogent ideas at this time, the interviewer will be very impressed. As medical director, you must be able to inspire others. Display this ability during your interview by being dynamic.

You may want to stress that these ideas are only preliminary and that you would want input from other major people at the facility before any of your plans are actually implemented.

As with all other topics, try to be flexible. Do not act as if you plan on entering the organization and taking over without a thought for the feelings of others. Emphasize that you value input from other physicians and employees. After all, many of them have been there for a long time and have useful experience regarding the facility and its operations. *Stress that you want to get to know the facility, its employees, and the community before you begin making any changes.*

BLUFFING WILL DOOM YOU

You will be asked very hard questions during your interview. In fact, the interviewer may ask you extremely hard questions to see how you handle the pressure of the situation. Don't try to bluff your way through answers. In all likelihood, you have good background knowledge in the topics that will be discussed during the interview. However, if a topic about which you do not know a great deal comes up, here's what to do. Try responding:

"I don't know that much about _____ because we don't deal

with that issue in my present position. However, I can guarantee you that if this is an important issue here, I'm a quick study and I'll make it a top priority to learn what I need to know in order to manage the situation in the best way possible."

If more information seems necessary, you might add an anecdote about something similar you've already grappled with and how well it's worked out.

WHAT TO DO WHEN YOU DISAGREE

Let's suppose the interviewer launches into a discussion, and you disagree with his or her viewpoint. Expressing your opinion is acceptable, and even advisable, when interviewing for a senior job; however, the manner in which you express your difference of opinion will be key in making a positive opinion.

Try to present your opinion in a neutral manner. For example, if the interviewer asserts that it is not a good idea for medical directors to sit in on hospital board meetings, you might want to say that the hospital for which you worked utilizes a different approach and found it helpful. You may want to explain what was good about the procedure and how it was helpful.

A good strategy for this type of discussion is to first confirm the validity of the interviewer's thought and then talk about contradictory evidence that you have experienced:

"That may be true for many hospitals, Dr. Smith, but when I worked for Americora Hospital, we allowed medical directors to sit in on meetings. We found that medical directors are often the employees who are most aware of the day-to-day functioning of the institution and usually contribute valuable input into meetings."

Without confronting (never use the words, "I disagree") and without putting the other person down, you have expressed a perfectly valid opinion. In this situation, your case is particularly strong because you are backing it up with personal experience about why you think having the directors sit in on the board meetings works.

Medical directors must have tact and social sensitivity, so it's important not to present information in a confrontational manner. Also, don't disagree with something that personally involved the interviewer or his job. In addition, do not disagree with his or her major concepts or beliefs.

Sometimes an interviewer may verbally attack you in an inappropriate manner. If this occurs, don't ignore it. Instead, calmly answer the question and comment that you have an alternate view. Remember, you must show that you can be assertive and not put up with unnecessary attacks from anyone.

IF THE INTERVIEWER CHALLENGES YOU

In contrast to the situation described above, where you may want to purposefully express opinions different than the interviewer, a circumstance may arise where an interviewer disagrees with one of your comments. In this situation, stay calm. The interviewer may have disagreed with you as a test to see how you handle pressure. The last thing you want to do is to look flustered or annoyed. First, politely confirm what the interviewer has said without showing any animosity. For example, in the situation discussed above, you might respond by saying:

"You think that medical directors should not be allowed to attend hospital board meetings? I would be interested in your experience and the reasons why you think this policy doesn't work."

You might then respond by agreeing with the basic concept of what the interviewer has said:

"I hadn't thought about the situation in that way before. In my experience at Americora Hospital, the system worked quite well."

At this point you should carefully weigh the reasons set forth by the interviewer. Based on these reasons, you can agree or disagree with the interviewer's stance. If the logic of his or her way of doing the job makes sense to you, acknowledge it and state that this would be a good way for future planning or practice.

Regardless of whether you decide to agree or disagree with the interviewer, make sure that you validate his or her point of view and then set forth your own reasons. Try to say it in a pleasant and friendly manner and avoid any sort of arguing.

FREQUENTLY ASKED QUESTIONS

As an applicant for a medical directorship, you will likely be asked many questions. Employers want someone who is tough and quick in responding to issues. One method interviewers sometimes use to ascertain this is to ask many rapid-fire questions. You definitely will not be handled with kid gloves during the medical directorship interview. Generally, interviewers will throw many questions at you to see how you handle the pressure.

Many questions with which you may be presented may not relate to past jobs and may catch you off guard (e.g., "What books have influenced you?"). These questions have a variety of purposes, including trying to get to know more about your personality and seeing how quickly you think. The key to these questions is to be honest. Don't respond with answers that are untrue and designed simply to impress the interviewer.

To help you prepare, we have devised a list of frequently asked questions. However, many other questions may also arise, and the overall impression interviewers have of your responses will make the difference between success and failure:

1. What is your current position and title?
2. What are your responsibilities?
3. What was your income in your last position?
4. What unique quality could you bring to our facility? (This question is particularly common. You should examine your characteristics in a circumspect manner to determine what unique qualities you embody that would help you as a director.)
5. How many employees did you supervise at the last facility at which you were employed?
6. Now that you have had a chance to see our operation and learn about the facility, what new ideas would you anticipate implementing if you are hired?
7. Why did you leave your last position? Or, why are you considering leaving your current position?
8. What do you think were your most important accomplishments in your last position?

9. What were some of the difficulties associated with this job and how did you manage to overcome them?
10. Tell me about some of the things that you have learned in your previous places of employment.
11. What did you like/dislike about your previous job?
12. Tell me about some of the tough decisions you have made in your previous job.
13. Have you had to fire employees? If so, how did you handle this situation?
14. Would you say that you are more of a micromanager or a macro-manager?
15. How do you think that employees who worked for you before might describe you?
16. What have you done within the last year to help yourself become a stronger leader?
17. What other positions are you considering?
18. What are some charities that interest you or in which you have participated?
19. What do you do in your spare time? What are your hobbies?
20. Describe your leadership style (i.e., authoritarian, democratic, etc.).

As can be seen by a quick inspection of these questions, many of them focus on the skills and responsibilities you had at your last place of employment. Employers rely very heavily on those aspects of your résumé and want to hear more about these factors during your interview.

EMBARRASSING QUESTIONS

Being put on the hot seat is par for the course when interviewing for a medical directorship. Many people refer to this type of interview as a stress interview, since the main goal may be to see how you handle the interview when it gets rough. One tactic that is sometimes used is to ask the job candidates embarrassing questions. While you may feel flustered or embarrassed and feel tempted to respond, "Hey! That's none of your business!" this will not go over well in an interview.

Instead, smile and try to come up with a more acceptable answer. Be as honest as you can, and the interviewer will admire your honesty and imperturbability. Take time to answer all questions that are posed. If you rush to answer the easy questions, your delay will be more evident when you are thrown for a loop by an unexpected or difficult question.

Here are some possible questions you might encounter:

1. Why should I hire you?
2. Aren't you overqualified/underqualified?
3. Why have you been out of work for some time?
4. Describe a time when your work has been criticized.
5. What were your previous boss's weak points?
6. What in your life would you do over if you could?
7. Why aren't you making more money by now?
8. How many hours a week do you normally work?
9. How could you have done better in your last position?
10. Tell me about something you did that makes you feel ashamed.
11. How long do you anticipate staying with this facility?
12. How do you feel about your progress to date?
13. Can we check your references?
14. Rate yourself on a scale from 1 to 10.
15. Tell me a story.

Most of these questions will probably not come up during a typical interview. However, be prepared just in case. Again, be honest and genuine. You can even laugh and explain that the question is interesting. Just try to answer it to the best of your ability.

A NOTE ABOUT WHAT YOU WEAR

As mentioned in chapter 3, job applicants are best advised to wear a simple tailored suit for an interview. However, as an applicant for a directorship position, it is especially important that you convey traits such as forcefulness, self-reliance, dynamism, aggressiveness, and decisiveness. As someone who has probably already had considerable success in your field, you know that you embody these attributes. The best way to convey this in your attire is in an authoritative manner—vertical lines, straight silhouettes, heavy textures, strong color contrasts, and dark colors. Though this may not reflect current fashion, it is the proper attire for an important interview.

Unspoken Gender Bias

Unfortunately, women may still encounter situations where they are interviewed by men who are convinced that it takes a man to do the job.

While barriers are coming down, you may feel frustrated to think that this may keep you from holding a job you want. The best advice is to persevere. While you may encounter a facility that prefers a man, this won't always be the case. If you keep at your job search, you'll find something that's right for you.

THE ℞ FOR DIRECTORSHIP SUCCESS

Being a medical director is a challenging job. Perhaps because of this, interviewers will often make these interviews tough and stressful.

Before your interview, take as much time as necessary to focus on qualities that make you unique. Be prepared to market yourself, your credentials, and your skills to get the job. During the interview, you have to be on your toes and assertive. However, the most important thing you must stress is the fact that you are unique and innovative.

The employers of the facility to which you are applying want the best person possible to run the organization. You have to convince the interviewers that you are the best candidate. Be confident in your quest for success.

- Prepare your cover letter carefully. This letter will be influential in determining if you receive the interview.
- Research the facility to which you are applying. Know the strengths and weaknesses of the organization and formulate a preliminary course of action.

- You will likely be interviewed by a panel. Be relaxed and remember that the more people who are present, the more important you are!
- Be assertive. Show that you will not let people walk all over you.
- Do not be apprehensive about discussing your managerial skills, such as organizational talent or delegating authority.
- Impress on the interviewer that you are devoted to your work and anticipate working long hours.
- You may be asked embarrassing questions. Do not become flustered and simply try to devise an adequate, possibly witty, answer. Always keep in mind that the interview is a stress test for you. Don't lose your cool.
- Don't ever say, "I disagree." Find a more tactful way to express your differing viewpoint.

14

GETTING "QUALIFIED": PREPARING FOR YOUR ORAL EXAM IN YOUR FIELD OF SPECIALTY

Board certification is usually the last step for you to achieve the highest level of qualification in medicine. If you pass the test, you can practice as a diplomate. Examiners want to make absolutely certain that you are qualified before you receive this honor.

Although some areas of medicine (e.g., internal medicine and pediatrics) include only a written examination, others have both a written and oral component (e.g., radiology, physical medicine and rehabilitation, neurology, and psychiatry). While there are numerous guides on preparing for board certification tests, this chapter will focus on how best to prepare for the oral portion of the exam. Although there are many differences between oral examinations for various disciplines, we will present guidelines that are helpful regardless of your area of discipline.

To qualify for an oral exam, you must first pass the written portion of your exam. Passing the written test is good preparation for your oral, as it indicates that you are proficient in your field of specialty.

It is highly recommended that you attend an oral board review course, which is generally held over a two-day period. The ideal time for taking the course is approximately one month before the exam, so be aware of when the sign-up date is so that you register in time for the session that will be right for you.

HOW DO YOU GET TO CARNEGIE HALL?

Practice, practice, practice. Like so many things in life, rehearsing is the key to passing your oral examination.

One good way to prepare for the exam is to use the guidelines laid out for your specialty as you see patients each day. By practicing what is preached, it will make the material seem like second nature, and if a practical interview is part of your examination, you'll be well prepared.

You'll also want to arrange for at least three mock interviews prior to your oral. If you know anyone who serves as an examiner for your board of specialty, he or she may be willing to help you out. And colleagues who have recently received board certification may also be very happy to help you. (Their comments may be particularly helpful since they've just been through it.)

While the prospect of making mistakes in front of your colleagues is a little unnerving, anyone who expresses willingness to help you will understand that this is all just a part of the learning process. They also recognize the significance of the exam; for that reason, many of your colleagues will almost certainly be willing to help you out.

After each mock exam, make notes about the feedback you receive so that you'll know where you need to make improvements.

BE CONFIDENT

Soon you will be dealing with patients on a regular basis and must seem certain of yourself and your knowledge of medicine, so the examiner is looking for candidates who display confidence. Don't be hesitant or take too long to answer questions. Present each answer in a confident manner (i.e., using a strong and even voice and without unnecessary pauses).

BE ARTICULATE

During the written part of the board exam, your knowledge in your field has been tested. During the oral exam, your verbal and interpersonal competence are at the forefront, and the clarity of your answer is very important.

Despite the fact that you will be nervous, try to concentrate on taking deep breaths and speaking slowly, without seeming rushed. (Some candidates are so nervous that they rush through their answers, and because they are speaking so quickly it is difficult to understand them.) If your answer is hurried, the examiner may conclude that your explanation is deficient, simply because he or she didn't have time to process it all.

Anxiety sometimes causes people to become flustered, and their answers become less clear. If you're feeling nervous, take a deep breath and regain your composure. Just because you had difficulty with one answer doesn't mean that you'll blow them all.

Try to use technical terms during the exam only if you are prepared to define them. The examiner may ask you to explain a term or a diagnosis that you have brought up. Being unable to sufficiently define a term that you have used will reflect poorly upon you.

APPEAR ORGANIZED

For many questions in medicine there is no single right answer, and that's one of the reasons why an organized reply is so important. If you muddle through a disorganized set of facts, it is unclear to the examiner whether or not you actually know the correct answer. However, if your answer is clear and organized, the examiner will be more likely to view your answer as correct.

As you study, note answers in bulleted or step-by-step points for the questions that you might potentially be asked. This will help you focus on the most important points. When you're actually in the oral examination situation, try to mentally perform the same task: For each answer, carefully but quickly outline the direction you are going to follow with your response. Touch upon each component of your answer and try to have a logical step-by-step presentation.

RELAX

Being nervous before your oral exam is perfectly natural—most people are. However, try to be as relaxed as possible, or it can affect your ability to do well. If you stay calm, you will be able to think in a clearer manner and will be more likely to formulate a suitable answer. If you seem excessively nervous, the examiner will be more likely to think that you are uncertain about your knowledge and may subsequently view you as an incompetent candidate.

Oral examinations are developed to help differentiate between people; as a result, some questions will be much more difficult than others. (Some will be almost impossibly hard.) Don't panic if you don't know an answer. It doesn't mean you won't be certified; other candidates will almost certainly hit roadblocks as well. If you're at a loss as to how to answer a question, it may be preferable to admit to the examiner that you have no idea how to answer this particular question. Making up answers will not generally help and may only serve to turn the examiner against you. Panicking will only make it harder for you to remember the answers to additional questions.

For suggestions on maintaining a relaxed state, refer to chapter 16, "Avoiding the Sweaty Palms Syndrome: Managing Your Anxiety."

YOU CATCH MORE FLIES WITH HONEY . . .

Think of the examiner as a colleague, not a superior, while simultaneously treating him or her with respect. As it happens, you may soon realize that you actually know more than the examiner does. You've been studying this area for many years and have had access to the most current data, while in contrast, your examiner took this test some time ago and may have forgotten some of it. Despite this, you most assuredly should avoid being arrogant or condescending during the interview, and even if you disagree with something that is said by the examiner, don't argue. Always remember that you are being evaluated by the examiner, not vice versa.

OLD "STONE FACE" ISN'T UNFRIENDLY; HE'S JUST DOING HIS JOB

Some candidates want to develop instant rapport with the examiner. However, the examiner is there only to administer the examination, not become your friend.

Most examiners conduct the oral exam with a "stone face" and will not be particularly responsive. They have been trained to act in this manner, and they attempt to be the same with each candidate. The examiner does not exhibit a reaction to your answers because she or he does not want you to know if you have given a correct or an incorrect answer. The examiner also wants to try to avoid giving nonverbal feedback to one candidate and not to another. However, this lack of responsiveness can be disconcerting, and all you can do is try to remind yourself not to take this lack of warmth personally.

Remember, too, that the examiner is not there to flunk you. He or she is there to help you get your board certification if you merit becoming a diplomate based on your knowledge and skill. So despite the "stone face" exterior, the examiner is rooting for you on the inside!

THE EXAMINATION PROCESS: WHAT TO EXPECT

In some specialties, such as psychiatry, the candidate is given a patient to examine and interview. Thus, the examinee must display her own interviewing skills, and present her findings and diagnostic impressions to the examiner afterward. You have to be as thorough as possible, but keep in mind that you will be working with time constraints.

Your patient interview time will pass quickly and you must use it wisely.

Normally, the examiner will bring the patient to you and introduce the two of you to each other. Be warm when you meet. Smile, shake hands with the patient, and introduce yourself if the examiner has not already introduced you. You may also want to thank the patient for agreeing to come for the interview. In addition, you should briefly explain the structure of the examination to the patient. Make it easier for the patient by telling her that you appreciate her help and will try to make the process easy.

For example, you can tell the patient that you will interview her for about half an hour (this is a common length for the psychiatry examination) or describe the type of examination procedures to be used. You might also say that you will be asking her a good number of questions, some of which she may have reviewed with others already. You might also let her know that some of the questions may not be relevant to her, may be hard to answer, or may even be somewhat embarrassing.

A common question with which to commence the interview is to inquire, "What brings you to the hospital?" This question is basically nonthreatening and allows the patient to begin with the most relevant material. Let the patient talk without interrupting her for the first few minutes. Then gradually you can keep the patient on track and prevent her from going off on tangents too often. Try to get as much information about the patient's current problem, as well as her personal health history.

During the examination period, it is vital that you display concern for the patient. Doctors must be altruistic and are expected to help their patients, so try to exhibit these qualities during your examination. Remember that the patient may be in pain (physical or emotional) and is experiencing some sort of trouble. What's more, the patient may be frightened or intimidated by the examination process itself.

Try to comfort the patient and make her feel at ease. It may be helpful to ask the patient if her illness has a name (i.e., What does she call her problem?). Also, have her explain what she thinks is wrong and what the causes of this problem might be. This information will make the patient feel as if she is helping you and also gives you insight into the patient's level of awareness about her condition.

Some candidates narrowly view the patient as just another exami-

nation item. These people appear as if they are using the patient to obtain the necessary information only. You would not want to be treated this way if you sought medical treatment. Also, when you are in practice you would not want to treat your patients in this manner. Therefore, you should not display this behavior during the examination. Do not rush through the examination; take all of the time allotted to you. Being systematic in your questioning will make the patient feel important and also allow you to be thorough.

The examiner might give you a warning that your time is nearly up (i.e., "You have five minutes left."). *Strictly adhere to this time limit.* If you go over, this could be very irritating to the examiner and you could automatically create a situation where he or she will be against you.

When you are finished with your examination, don't rush the patient to leave. Ask if she has any questions for you, and be sure to thank the patient for allowing you to talk to her. Anytime that you interact with a patient, you are a representative of the entire discipline of medicine. Conducting yourself well is very important.

CONDUCTING A VIDEO ANALYSIS

The use of videotapes during the certification process is becoming more and more popular. In psychiatry, for example, the live patient interview is followed by a videotape of a patient that a group of candidates will watch for about ten minutes. The candidates must then proffer brief presentations concerning the taped patient.

In this presentation, discuss your findings, differential diagnosis, probable diagnosis, and treatment recommendations. Given that you will have limited data about the patient, don't make too many unfounded hypotheses. Try to be broad and somewhat general in your recommendations and conclusions.

PRESENTATION TO THE EXAMINER

During the case presentation, there will generally be two examiners present. However, a third person (senior examiner) may drop by for a few minutes and observe the examination process or ask a few questions. When you are presenting the case, refer to the patient as Ms. or Mr. _____, showing warmth by using the proper name as well as respect by not calling the patient "Carol" or "Dave." Also refrain from speaking of the patient using cold or overly clinical references.

Begin the presentation with a discussion of the patient's identifying information, reason for referral, primary presenting problem, past history, medical problems, family history, and current status.

Conscientiously deliberate and discuss the differential diagnoses, taking into account the entire repertoire of symptoms exhibited by the patient. Formulate sound reasons for ruling out and ruling in particular diagnoses. In general, the more complete you are when addressing the differential diagnosis, the more impressed the examiner will be.

End your presentation with a consideration concerning potential treatments that could be employed.

Never say anything negative about the patient, even in jest, and stress the patient's strengths. You can do this in the beginning of your presentation. For example, you may comment that the patient was friendly, cooperative, good-natured, or any other positive adjectives that may be appropriate. When presenting your material, it is often a good idea to start with these assets first.

Overall, try to present the material in a rational and coherent manner and construct a clear outline. Being systematic during the examination with the patient will help you be systematic during your case presentation. In actuality, the skill with which you present your case and the propriety you display with the patient will be as important as your knowledge during the oral examination.

A board examiner in neurology once explained the main reason that he had flunked a particular candidate. The examinee performed very well on the oral section, giving near-perfect answers to each question. However, during the physical/neurological examination, the candidate pulled up the female patient's shirt in a rough and embarrassing way and without advance notice. This incident made the patient feel uncomfortable, and thus resulted in the examinee failing the examination. The candidate's bedside manner was severely lacking. Because this quality is considered so significant to a doctor's success in dealing with patients, the examiner thought that the absence of this attribute should result in a lack of certification, despite superior knowledge.

Qualifying at Your Orals: The ℞

- Practice answering questions orally in your office or at home. You may feel silly, but this technique will help you prepare.
- Be confident! You have tremendous knowledge concerning your specialty.
- Be organized and articulate in your presentation.
- Be relaxed!
- Don't be put off by an emotionless examiner. They are instructed to conduct the exam in that way in order to be as fair and impartial as possible with each candidate.
- If part of your oral exam involves interviewing a real patient, be respectful and warm.

PART THREE

PERFECTING THE ART OF THE INTERVIEW

15

"I DIDN'T SAY THAT, *DID* I?" MISTAKES PEOPLE MAKE WHEN INTERVIEWING

In almost every interview, you'll find that there will be at least one heart-pounding moment when you think, *"What* should I say?" or "What *did* I say?" both leading to the conclusion that you may never get this job.

As you know, that kind of thinking is all just a part of the nervousness of job-hunting, and when all is said and done, the things you worried about weren't a particularly big deal after all. However, because there are some mistakes that most applicants make at some time or another, this chapter will sum up the most common ones and recommend ways you may be able to avoid making the mistake at all.

AVOIDING THE "MAD ABOUT ME" SYNDROME

Interviews can be difficult because you want to present your best qualities and dazzle the interviewer while you simultaneously avoid boasting about your accomplishments. There is a fine line between marketing yourself and bragging.

When discussing your strengths, talk about what others have told you. For example, if you are a hard worker, explain to the interviewer that your friends, colleagues, or former supervisors have often said that you work very hard. If prepared well, your letters of recommendation will make note of your strengths, so do not try too hard during most interviews to market yourself (a notable exception being the medical director interview). Bragging will only taint your image and minimize the esteem that the interviewer has for you.

"YES, NO, MAYBE SO?" DEVELOPING A SENSE OF APPROPRIATENESS

Most questions that you will be asked during your interview will be open-ended, meaning that you will be responsible for determining what topics are covered and the length of your response. Nervousness in applicants generally comes out in two ways: they are either too long-winded, or they can barely cough out a yes or a no. Neither is appropriate. Rambling or verbose answers may bore the interviewer. Likewise, answers consisting of only a few terse words (e.g., yes or no responses) are inadequate. In this case, you may be viewed as taciturn and lacking in interpersonal skills.

The best advice for judging the proper length of your answers is to relax enough once you're in the situation so that you can pick up on the clues that are given to you by the interviewer. Every question will require an answer of a different length, so there is no set formula.

Begin by making sure you adequately cover the relevant topics. Then start looking for cues. If the interviewer is tapping his pencil, looking at his watch, or ruffling papers, or if his eyes look glazed over, you need to tighten up your answers. However, if she appears to be relaxed and is nodding or smiling or asks a follow-up question, this is your cue to continue providing information.

SHOW YOUR ENTHUSIASM

Some applicants display a cool attitude and act as if they do not need the position. This attitude may be mistaken for a lack of interest. Sometimes an applicant assumes that the interviewer knows that he is really interested in the job, but this is a mistaken assumption. The interviewer may speculate that you already have several offers or you are applying at many other places. Therefore, you always need to demonstrate enthusiasm for the position. An interviewer wants to hire someone who *really* wants to work at this particular facility.

ECCENTRICS CAN ONLY LOOK ECCENTRIC AFTER THEY GET THE JOB

The wild-haired scientist or the harried doctor, too busy to tuck in his shirttail, must have developed these habits only after landing the job. Despite the fact that your qualifications and your dedication to work are what should get you the job, appearances do count. As a physician and professional, you will be a representative of the particular organization to which you belong, so you must look proper during every phase of the interview. One board-certified radiologist was turned down during his first job interview because his shirt was not pressed! People may assume (as they did in this case) that if you present with disheveled clothing or slovenly hygiene during your interview, then your work may be careless or slipshod. Even if you apply for a position in which you will not deal with the public, you must still display suitable attire and hygiene. Refer to chapter 3 for guidelines.

AVOIDING THE "TABOO" SUBJECTS

There are two important subjects that should be avoided: politics and religion. Although these topics may be brought up by the interviewer, you should tactfully avoid addressing them.

Avoiding politics means steering away from conversations about things like which candidates you might support or oppose, the political party you endorse, and opinions about the current presidential administration and its policies. However, politics also includes such hot issues as abortion, assisted suicide, sex education or prayer in schools, and health care reform. Because people in this country have such varying opinions on such issues, you run the risk of offending or alienating someone if you discuss your own views.

Religion is another private matter that should not be discussed. Religion is a matter that is followed based on faith and thus cannot necessarily be logically defended by people. Discussing such an issue is asking for trouble. In fact, even identifying your own religious background should be avoided because, again, you may alienate certain people. Your main goal during interviews is to have everyone like you in order to increase your likelihood of getting the position.

You should also avoid making jokes that poke fun of any group of people or any beliefs. You will never know if a joke you are telling would offend someone.

DESPERATELY SEEKING WORK . . .

Seeking a position in the medical field can be very stressful. Due to economics, population factors, and the rise of managed care, most positions are increasingly competitive, so you may feel desperate—but you really can't act that way. Don't be pushy about receiving the position, and never beg. Interviewers see these acts as signs of helplessness and a lack of self-respect, qualities not wanted in an employee or colleague. And if you are the right candidate and would have received the position anyway, you also don't want to step into it with people feeling sorry for you. Display confidence; let them see that you are the best candidate for the placement.

SWEATY PALMS, POUNDING HEART

Everyone is nervous during interviews. Indeed, a moderate amount of nervousness may actually allow you to attain an optimal interview performance. However, being too nervous will prevent you from succeeding during an interview, and may even make your interviewer feel uncomfortable because you are.

Interviewers prefer candidates that are confident and can enter interpersonal situations with ease. Try to be relaxed and confident in your responses. Smiling also may help you appear less nervous. See chapter 16 for additional suggestions.

ACCENTUATE THE POSITIVE AND MINIMIZE THE NEGATIVE

Frequently, candidates will be negative during an interview without even realizing it. For example, the interviewer may ask you about your relationship with a previous supervisor. If you didn't get along well with this supervisor, don't complain. Try to concentrate on the supervisor's good qualities. The guy might have been on your back all the time about getting things done, but your comment might be, "Tom was a terrific time manager. He kept track of all the details of the department and always made sure that things got done." You needn't exaggerate and say that he was the most wonderful person you ever knew, but don't say that you didn't like him.

If you had significant disagreements with a former supervisor, and you think this might come up if they check with your previous employers, you may want to explain that you did not agree on all issues, but that you always worked hard to do your job well. Remember that an employer is not going to want to hire someone who doesn't get along well with others.

Avoid using the word "hate" during your interview. In general, you should look for positive aspects of any situation to talk about in the interview.

MONEY, MONEY, MONEY?

While a financial discussion is an important part of any job negotiation, it is a mistake to try to talk specifics too early. Until the interviewer begins to imply that an offer is being made, applicants should not discuss such matters in detail.

But applicants have the right to get some idea of what kind of money is on the table. Try asking something like, "Can you give me a ballpark figure as to what this position is likely to pay?" However, during the interview is not the time to begin asking about perks or negotiating salary.

Never indicate that the salary has led you to the job. Sometimes when applicants are asked why they are applying for a certain position, they respond by saying that the position pays well. Even if this is true, this answer is not a good one. Interviewers perceive this as being greedy. They may also believe that you will require many raises and may prematurely leave if offered another position elsewhere that pays better. In general, it is best to talk about money issues as little as possible during the interview. Once the job has been offered you, you can then begin to talk specifics—many of your questions regarding benefits are likely better discussed with the personnel office, anyway.

THE ℞ FOR AVOIDING CLASSIC MISTAKES

- Don't brag. Let the good news about you come out in a variety of ways, including your letters of recommendation.
- Answer appropriately. If you confine yourself to yes and no answers, or if you ramble, you're not putting your best foot forward.
- Express enthusiasm for the job; a laid-back approach is viewed as no interest.
- Be eccentric *after* you get the job.
- Avoid discussion of religion or politics.
- Never act desperate.
- If you're too anxious, you'll make the interviewer anxious as well. If you're prone to nervousness, refer to chapter 16 for methods to help you interview better.
- Be positive in all your replies.
- Don't enter into a money discussion too soon. Wait until it's clear that a job is going to be offered to you.

16

AVOIDING THE SWEATY PALMS SYNDROME: MANAGING YOUR ANXIETY

Your heart races, you feel light-headed, your palms are sweating profusely... What's going on here? An encounter with a grizzly bear? No, just an encounter with a job interviewer.

Don't worry. Your reaction is normal—but unsettling all the same. Most people experience a great deal of stress during the interview process. This stress is appropriate and may actually help your performance by keeping you alert and on your toes.

However, some people experience so much stress that it becomes overwhelming and may destroy their performance. For that reason, this chapter contains some techniques that may be used to help you deal with anxiety. Lowering your stress before, during, and after an interview will allow you to perform at your peak level of achievement.

Finally, we hope that if you can relax during the interview process, you can enjoy it more. Indeed, although interviews elicit anxiety in most people, those who manage to relax report that they enjoy being interviewed and talking about themselves.

IDENTIFYING STRESS

Most people think that it is easy to identify stress. If you ask them to describe what it feels like, however, they generally have a difficult time describing the experience. Some may describe stress as simply having too many things to do and not enough time to do them. Others may describe stress through their bodily symptoms, such as a headache or an upset stomach.

Neither answer is wrong. They are just incomplete. Having too much to do is a cause of stress, and the symptoms described are the physical manifestations of stress. What's more, stress is unique to each person and manifests itself in various guises.

Generally, researchers talk about three main components of anxiety or stress: physiological, behavioral, and cognitive.

1. **Physiological symptoms.** For a long time now, clinicians have acknowledged that stress affects our bodies and our physical health. Therefore, if a person is under great stress, his or her immune system is overworked, and this may allow an illness to occur. Many people who are stressed report having headaches, stomachaches, nausea, or butterflies in their stomach. Other common symptoms of anxiety and worry include trembling, shakiness, restlessness, difficulty concentrating, difficulty breathing, dry mouth, sweaty/clammy palms, dizziness, light-headedness, hot flashes or chills, trouble swallowing, jumpiness or hypervigilance, fatigue, trouble sleeping, muscle tension or aches, pounding or racing heart, or heart palpitations.
2. **Behavioral symptoms** of stress are what people actually do to try to rid themselves of their stress. For example, many people may wring their hands or pull their hair. Others may try to leave the situation that makes them stressed (for example, leaving a high school reunion early or refusing to take an airplane). This behavior can be troubling because sometimes people become phobic about places that make them feel stressed; by avoiding those places, they can effectively disrupt their normal lives. For example, if Nancy gets stressed out because she does not have a lot of money and begins to avoid going to the bank so she does not have to think about her financial problems, this could interfere with her life and lead to her not doing things she should or wants to do. If Joe gets exceedingly anxious about going for a job interview, he may stay home instead of actively seeking a job.
3. **Cognitive symptoms** of stress are the thoughts that people have when they encounter a lot of stress. Usually, most people who are stressed worry a lot of the time. One type of worrisome thought is

called catastrophizing. People who catastrophize think a lot about "What if . . ." The thought, "What if I say something stupid?" is usually followed by a sequence of imagined and unrealistic consequences.

For example, a job candidate might think, "What if I stumble over my words during the interview?" Next, she thinks about the consequences of this action and falsely assumes, "The interviewer will think that I am stupid." This thought is followed by another assumption: "If he thinks I am stupid, he will not give me this job." The next thought in this chain might be, "If I do not get this job, I will never get a job." The downward spiral continues as the applicant assures herself that if she does not get a job, "I will be a failure and no one will ever like me." A simple fear of saying something wrong leads to a string of horrible consequences and makes the applicant feel fearful and anxious.

The Easiest Stress-Buster of All: Deep Breathing

If you are like most people, breathing deeply and slowly and speaking in an even tone will help your body relax, and you will automatically feel less stressed. This technique makes you focus on your body and slow it down. In addition, the increased oxygen from deep breathing helps you think more clearly and feel better.

COPING METHODS

Fortunately, many methods of coping with anxiety and stress have been developed. We have included a section on some coping methods that have proven to be effective in treating more severe anxiety problems.

Relaxation

The most commonly used method for helping people deal with their stress and anxiety is relaxation. This method, an exercise recommended by M. G. Craske, D. H. Barlow, and T. O'Leary in *Mastery of Your Anxiety and Worry,* is one that can be quite simple and effective.

Most people assume that they know how to relax. For example, some people may like to relax by watching a football game or reading a good novel. This kind of relaxation is *mental relaxation*. Participating in activities we enjoy is relaxing mentally because we have fun and can forget our problems. However, *muscle relaxation* is very different.

Most people cannot tell whether their muscles are tense or relaxed. Progressive muscle relaxation shows an individual how to relax their muscles in order to identify the differences between relaxation and tension. The muscle exercises involve tensing and releasing muscles in various muscle groups.

Generally, you should be in a quiet, dark room in a reclining position. Make sure that you are not going to be disturbed. This part of the exercise is the mental relaxation. For the muscle relaxation, start at the top of your body and tense the muscles, hold tension, and then release the muscles. To help you in this process, a step-by-step explanation is included.

After you have practiced the technique and have gotten good at it, you can utilize parts of it on the way to an interview (while on the airplane or taking public transportation to the facility).

Instructions. Choose a quiet, secluded room in which you can practice this technique without interruption. Put on comfortable, nonrestrictive clothes and remove your shoes. You may wish to dim the lights so that the room is darkened to a restful level. Then, position your body in a reclining posture that you find comfortable. Lying on your bed or sitting in a comfortable chair is ideal. Close your eyes and sit quietly for a minute or so to adjust to the conditions before you start the exercise. (For the times listed below, do not use a stopwatch. Instead, count in your head or use estimates.)

1. Start with your hands. Ball your hands into fists with your fingers in your palms, and close your hands tightly. Feel the tension that is created and the sensation of your muscles tightening. Focus on the tightness in your lower arms, wrists, fingers, knuckles, and hands. Hold your fists taut for 5 seconds, then tighten your fists again. Notice that your muscles pull and the tension increases in your muscles. Note to yourself how this feels.
   You should hold the tension for another 5 seconds and then

tighten your fists yet again and note the tension increasing. Release your fists quickly. Lay your hands down on the chair or bed. Concentrate on how your hands feel. What does it feel like to release the tension and relax? Some people's hands feel warm and relaxed after the release. Other people feel a tingling sensation. Whatever it feels like for you, concentrate on this feeling. Relax your hands for 20 seconds before you move to the next step.

2. Now, tense your arms by pulling them tightly to your side with the palms touching your legs. Your shoulders and back should be straight. You may feel like a tin soldier. Feel the tension in your arms and back. Continue this exercise for 5 seconds and then tighten your arms at your side. After another 5 seconds, release your muscle tension and let your arms fall loosely at your side. Focus on the sensations and how your arms feel in a relaxed state. Relax your arms for 20 seconds and then proceed to step 3.

3. Next, tense your lower legs. Flex your legs so that they are straight. Now point your toes up toward the ceiling (or toward your head if you are lying down). Feel the tension disperse through your feet, ankles, shins, and calf muscles. Focus on the tightness of your muscles for 5 seconds and then tighten the muscles further in your legs. Hold for another 5 seconds. Release and allow your legs to relax for 20 seconds. Again, concentrate on the sensation of relaxation in your legs.

4. Your upper legs are the next target for relaxation. Place your knees together and begin to lift your legs off the chair or bed. Pull your legs toward your stomach. Focus on the pulling sensations in your thigh and upper leg muscles. Hold this position for 10 seconds. Release the tension and let your legs down onto the chair or bed. Relax for 20 seconds while concentrating on these relaxed feelings.

5. The stomach will be tensed in this step. Pull in your stomach. Don't just suck in your breath, but use your stomach muscles. Pretend that you are trying to make your stomach touch your spine. Feel the tension in the muscles as you pull. Feel the warmth radiate through your abdominal area. Hold the tension for 5 seconds and then hold for another 5 seconds before releasing. Relax for 20 seconds and feel the comfort of the relaxation.

6. Next, work on your shoulders. Pull your shoulders toward the sides of your neck. Your shoulders will probably almost touch your ears.

Focus on your shoulders and the feeling of tension that swells through them. Hold this tension for 5 seconds, then tighten your shoulders again for another 5 seconds. Let your shoulders droop and feel the relaxation. Let your shoulders relax for 20 seconds, then try step 7.

7. Press the back of your neck against the chair or bed. Keeping your neck straight, pull your chin to your chest and constrict the muscles. Focus on the tightness in your neck and back. Hold for 10 seconds and release. Place the back of your head against the back of the chair so that your head is being held up by the chair. Relax in this manner for 20 seconds.
8. The next focus for relaxation is your jaw. Clench your teeth together tightly. Then, pull the corners of your mouth back in an exaggerated smile. You may feel like a grimacing jack-o'-lantern. Hold for 5 seconds and then tighten the muscles again. Maintain this tension for an additional 5 seconds. Release the tension and relax for 20 seconds.
9. Your face muscles will be the last group that you will tense. Specifically, you will tighten your upper and lower forehead muscles. Pull your eyebrows together and down toward your eyes so that your forehead furrows. Hold for 10 seconds and then release. Relax for 20 seconds and concentrate on the feelings in your forehead. Next, pull your eyebrows apart from each other and raise them toward the top of your head and hold for 10 seconds. When you relax the muscles, once again note the feelings in your forehead. Rest for 20 seconds.

At this point, your entire body should be relaxed and feel comfortable. Count from one to five and feel yourself become even more relaxed. Concentrate on your breathing. Make your breathing steady and slow. Every time you breathe in or out, repeat the word "relax" in your head. Stay in this state for as long as you desire. To become more alert, count backward from five to one.

When you complete this exercise and have practiced it several times, you may find the parts of your body where you most often manifest stress. For example, one candidate found that when his jaw tightened up it made the rest of his body feel tense as well. By using these techniques, he was able to feel relaxed. You can focus on particular muscles, or you can do the entire exercise. Much will depend on the availability of time and a quiet place for you to do the exercise. Of course, you need to use caution when employing this exercise and discontinue it if any pain occurs.

After you practice for a time, you will find it much faster and easier to relax your muscles, and you will soon be able to use the technique on the way to an interview.

A Safe Place

To combat stress, some people have what they call a "safe place." This is an imaginary scene that they use in order to feel more relaxed during stressful situations. For example, when Mary is feeling really stressed, she might imagine that she is alone on a beautiful beach drinking a fancy drink that has an umbrella in it and listening to the waves gently wash onto the shore.

People use this type of imaginary safe place to escape and relax. If you decide to use this technique, spend some time in advance of any interviews thinking through what your safe place should be. Choose some place where you could relax totally. This might be a familiar setting, like your kitchen or bedroom, that you associate with feeling relaxed. Or it might be a fantasy location like an isolated beach or a mountain cabin. Some people select places that are tranquil (like a beach); others choose places where they would be doing something they love, like playing golf or riding horseback.

Regardless of the safe place you select, make sure you give it as much detail as possible. Think of what the place smells like, what sounds you can hear, whether you are alone or with someone else. What are you doing? You might want to be napping or hitting tennis balls. The important thing is to feel happy and relaxed when you visualize this place. Then you can escape to it when you begin to feel overly nervous because your interviewers have kept you waiting for a half hour or when you're particularly stressed.

Desensitization

For this technique, you need to sit down and brainstorm about what specifically makes you tense, nervous, or scared about interviews. It is imperative that you be as specific as possible. For example, many people feel very nervous about meeting the interviewer. Other people may be afraid of being asked hard questions. Try to think of at least 10 things about the interview that make you feel nervous.

After this task has been accomplished, rank the items in order of severity, listing the easiest or least stress-provoking item at the top of the list and the hardest or most stress-provoking item at the bottom of the list. For each item, try to provide as much detail as possible.

Once you can easily attain a state of relaxation, the relaxed state is paired with items from the fear hierarchy. Start your relaxation by completing the progressive muscle relaxation exercises described above. Then, imagine the first (easiest) item on your hierarchy. You may begin to feel nervous or stressed. Try to think about the item for as long as you can until you become too nervous. Then, let the item leave your mind and try to relax again. If necessary, do your exercises again to help you relax. Once you obtain a state of relaxation, you can think of that item again.

Continue this process until you can think about this item without feeling nervous, or at least without feeling excessive nervousness or fear. Accomplishing this feeling may take several sessions of relaxation and imaginal exposure. Don't feel bad if it takes awhile, and be sure to work at your own pace. Basically, this procedure ends when you can think about each item on your fear hierarchy with moderate levels of stress. If necessary, you may wish to construct another fear hierarchy with new items that you did not think of before. Simply reapply the above procedures.

Stress Inoculation Training

Developed by Dr. Donald Meichenbaum, stress inoculation training (SIT) does not consist of a single technique. Instead, there are several components. Basically, SIT was designed to help the individual develop "psychological antibodies" to stress. These antibodies consist of coping methods that help people deal with future sources of stress. (The name SIT was chosen because of the technique's similarities to medical inoculation.)

We have adapted the SIT method for use by applicants. For a complete description of SIT, however, the reader is encouraged to refer to Meichenbaum's work. Here are the most relevant coping methods advocated by SIT.

Self-monitoring. This is a technique in which people keep track of how many times they have certain thoughts, perform certain behaviors, or experience certain feelings. As we discussed before, many people are not able to identify stress. We recommend self-monitoring because it can help you become better at identifying stress. There are a number of ways that one can use self-monitoring to accomplish this goal. For example, if you tend to have a lot of headaches when you are stressed, you can self-monitor your headaches. Below, we outline the steps of self-monitoring.

1. Carefully define the target behavior. Using our example from above, you may want to define a headache as any head pain that is severe enough to require taking a pain reliever (aspirin, acetaminophen, ibuprofen).

    If you deal with stress by avoiding things that make you stressed, you can self-monitor this behavior. You may want to specifically define avoidance as abstaining from initiating conversations because you fear making mistakes in front of other people.
2. Decide how you want to record the occurrence of the behavior. You may wish to carry a small pad and note each time it happens. Another commonly used and more discreet method is to use a golf counter. You can place the golf counter in your pocket and simply tap the button each time you wish to record a behavior, thought, or feeling. (Golf counters are fairly inexpensive and can be obtained at most sporting goods stores.)

    It may also be a good idea to record what happens before and after the behavior, thought, or feeling. Recording this information will help you determine the circumstances under which you feel stress.
3. Keep accurate records of your self-monitoring. This will allow you

to determine if your stress has been reduced as you continue through the other steps. Also, you will become more aware of when, where, and how you exhibit the symptoms of stress.

Relaxation training. Use the techniques of relaxation training described above for this method. As can be seen, relaxation training is commonly used in many stress reduction programs.

Be Prepared

As simple as this advice may sound, perhaps the easiest and most effective method for dealing with stress is to be properly prepared. If you feel that you know what to expect, you will enter the interview with less stress. Being prepared will make you feel more confident and able to handle whatever is thrown your way. Ask a colleague, a trusted individual, or other professional to give you one or more practice interviews. Tell them to be as realistic as possible.

Although these practice interviews will of course not be exactly like the real thing, practicing will allow you to get a feel for what an actual interview will be like. Also, realize that the absolute worst thing that can happen is that you may not receive the position that you want. Although the failure to obtain a position is indeed a negative outcome, you can deal with this failure and try again.

Think Positive

During a stressful interview, you may find it helpful to use positive coping statements. These are simple statements that put a positive outlook on the stress you're enduring. Simply put, you're talking to yourself, telling yourself that you will get the job, and assuring yourself that you will do a great job during the interview. Before the interview, think of things you can say to yourself that will help you feel positive. The suggestions below may help:

- I have succeeded in job interviews before.
- I am qualified for this job.
- I am calm.

- I interview well.
- People find me pleasant.
- I am relaxed.
- My résumé looks good.
- I can do this job.
- This interview will be over soon.
- I like talking about myself.
- I am an intelligent person and that shines through.
- I will get this job.
- I am well prepared for this job because I did my homework and read *The Physician's Job-Search ℞*!

THE ℞ FOR RELAXATION

- Practice the relaxation exercise provided.
- Practice the desensitization exercise provided.
- Practice stress inoculation training by monitoring your stress level and identifying how you cope when you feel stressed. By noticing the stressor and the stress reaction, you can use SIT to begin to relax.
- Create a "safe place" where you can escape mentally when you begin to feel particularly stressed.
- Breathe deeply when you're under stress. This will slow you down and make you feel more relaxed.
- Give yourself a pep talk. That will make you feel more positive—and more relaxed—during the interview.

Experiment with these methods to see which one works best for you. If none of these methods provide significant relief for your anxiety related to being interviewed, you may wish to consider consulting an expert clinician or your family doctor.

17

SPECIAL TIPS FOR SPECIAL SITUATIONS: OVERCOMING POSSIBLE OBSTACLES

No doubt about it. There are lots of unfair reasons people don't get jobs. While the U.S. government has made many efforts to try to create an atmosphere in which jobs must be offered equally to all, it isn't 100 percent successful. One of the reasons is that much of what happens in hiring is subconscious. Few people set out to be discriminatory, but when they think about adding an important person to their workplace, someone whom they must come to trust and depend upon, they often gravitate to someone who is much like themselves or much like someone they know well. The result, of course, is the perpetuation of sameness in the workforce, reducing opportunities for people who—because of their race, gender, nationality, or some type of handicap—are perceived as less likely to fit in.

Given the difficulties inherent in attaining a job in the medical field, it probably comes as no surprise that those in special populations may face special obstacles in this process. In this section, we will discuss some specific techniques that can be used to help people who belong to these groups attain the medical job they desire.

Discrimination vs. Bias?
Although many laws exist that attempt to abolish discrimination in hiring practices, it is difficult to believe that it does not exist to

> some extent. Though interviewers may attempt to be unbiased about an applicant's status, they may still hold biases that are unconscious and unintentional.
>
> The short-term solution is doing such a great job in the interview that you are irresistible to them; the long-term solution is community-wide consciousness-raising, which includes—but is not limited to—getting hired, doing a great job, and thereby breaking yet one more cultural stereotype barrier.
>
> Refer to chapter 18 for additional advice on questions that may be discriminatory (and therefore, illegal).

COPING WITH A PHYSICAL DISABILITY

The Vocational Rehabilitation Act of 1973 makes it illegal for persons with a physical handicap to be discriminated against based on factors that do not have a direct bearing on her or his ability to perform the job. However, persons with disabilities still face special challenges when seeking employment in medicine.

In the *Journal of Applied Social Psychology,* there appeared a report on a study concerning the hiring of people with visible disabilities. The study started off with subjects hearing an audiotaped mock interview. In one of the taped interviews, an applicant disclosed that he was disabled. In the other, the same applicant did not disclose such a disability. It was found that subjects rated the disabled applicants higher than the able-bodied applicants on measures of honesty, ambition, intelligence, creativity, cooperation, and being a hard worker. However, when subjects stated who they would hire, the able-bodied applicants were more frequently picked! Even though interviewers may have sympathy for a person with a disability and view positively their favorable traits, a bias still remains against these applicants. The underlying fear may be that the interviewers worry that a disabled worker may be unable to perform certain tasks, including ones that he or she may actually be able to complete very competently.

Unfortunately, people generally allow negative information to carry more weight than positive information. Thus, persons with a handicap must not only display the skills necessary for a given job, but must also focus on impressing the interviewer even more than other applicants.

Here are some suggestions for success:

1. Though this is somewhat controversial, it is our belief that you needn't disclose your disabled status until the interview. If you are fully capable of performing the job for which you are applying, then your disability is immaterial. Once you're in the door, you'll have a better opportunity to prove your point. You want to procure the position based on your qualifications while simultaneously bypassing unfair biases that may arise against you due to your status.

    Though some interviewers may react negatively to being caught off guard, others may recognize within themselves their bias in assuming that all applicants were able-bodied. Those that recognize this will likely continue the interview with an open mind.

    Prior to the interview, focus on presenting a good application and performing well during the telephone preinterview. The interviewer will then remember more positive and desirable aspects of you, such as your sense of humor or your eloquence, and that will get you off to a good start at the in-person interview.

2. Focus on your strengths. Explain to the interviewer past experience you have in the medical field or your record in medical school or during residency. Be as specific as possible during this discussion. Before your interview, write down the qualities that make you unique. For example, you may be unusually creative, have a great deal of patience, or be an expert on a particular medical topic. Be able to discuss these qualities with the interviewer, stressing how you will use these elements within the job.

3. During the interview itself, you will want to address your disability. (At some point you need to help the interviewer overcome any doubts he or she might have about your ability to do the work.) Depending on the nature of your impairment, talk about what you've done to overcome any difficulties you've encountered. If you work directly with patients, you might tell an anecdote about how patients react. (If you work with children, you may have some amusing anecdotes about their questions or some interesting anecdotes about how you handle it if they show any fear.)

4. Address your attendance record. This falls into the category of staving off underlying biases that interviewers may not even realize they have. Certainly one stereotype of people with disabilities is that they may be ill more frequently than others, or they may need time off because of ongoing medical needs. If you stress that you've rarely missed a day in your previous job, that makes the interviewer aware that you are healthy, conscientious, and place a high priority on your work.
5. Maintain your sense of humor. Seeking a position is a difficult task for everyone. Because of your handicap, this chore may sometimes be overwhelming. In addition, you may encounter people who treat you with a lack of respect.

    You have two options—become disheartened and give up your search, or keep a sense of humor and be persistent. Be proud of your ability to persevere under adversity and you will eventually triumph.

OBESITY

Several studies have demonstrated that people who are obese (technically defined as 20 percent over the "ideal" weight) often face bias when they are seeking jobs.

In *Social and Work Occupations,* authors J. C. Larkin and H. A. Pines examined the effects of obesity on hiring decisions made by college-age subjects. The participants were asked to state which of two mock job applicants—one obese and the other of normal weight—they would prefer. Two job-related tasks were performed by the applicants, but the subjects viewed only the applicants' hands during the process. Consistently, the two applicants (obese and non-obese) were judged as equal in quality of task performance. However, despite this equivalence, when the test takers were asked to select one of them for the job, they were less likely to hire the applicant who was obese.

In a similar study (published in the *International Journal of Obesity*), the same result was replicated, and the study went on to examine prejudices against the obese: across the board, the obese job applicants were viewed as exhibiting poorer work habits than persons who were of normal weight; they were viewed as more likely to have absences from work that were not caused by medical problems; and they were judged to be late more often, and to abuse company privileges via fabricating illness more frequently, than persons without obesity. In addition, the applicants who were obese were evaluated by subjects as being less likely to get along well with other people, lacking in self-control and discipline, and as generally lonely, depressed, and anxious. Overall, the authors concluded that "the most surprising results were the strong negative attitudes held about the overweight applicants' interpersonal skills and problems."

If you fear that you may encounter this sort of unfair bias, here are some guidelines that will allow you to present yourself well during the interview process:

1. Dress well. There are an increasing number of stores and departments within larger stores that are geared to the plus-size market, and some designers are even featuring clothing aimed for larger people. Like every other applicant, it is important that you have a terrific-looking interview suit or outfit, so take the time to find something that fits properly and looks good on you.

    While both sexes should stick to conservative colors for the suit, women can brighten their attire with a great scarf or a cheerfully colored blouse. The days of the black caftan look are gone. Take a stand and dress proudly. You're a doctor or ready to be a doctor, and that's definitely something about which to be proud. With their business suit, men can add a tie that is interesting but still businesslike—a pediatrician can probably get away with something a bit more lighthearted.

    If you seem comfortable and confident, that will put your interviewer at ease as well. See chapter 3 for further details concerning proper attire.
2. Remain enthusiastic during your interview. Be positive and keep your energy level high. Remember that although it is unfounded, many interviewers view people who are obese as lazy or lacking in energy.
3. Focus on your achievements and the hard work that was necessary for you to attain your accomplishments. By establishing that you have a strong work ethic and a desire to achieve as part of a team,

you ought to be able to even the playing field so that you have an equal opportunity for the job you seek.

As with any condition that may cause bias against you, presenting yourself well during the interview will enable you to overcome these prejudices and attain the position you desire.

THE AFRICAN AMERICAN CANDIDATE

In medicine today, the qualified African American candidate should not face many insurmountable obstacles, and he or she will likely find that almost everybody is happy to have an African American among their colleagues. While this is not to say that there won't be isolated occurrences of discrimination, in all likelihood you'll find the job market quite receptive to you if you're African American, and you'll be hired as quickly as any other graduate.

However, native African graduates with foreign accents will find the market as tough as for any other international graduates. The advice below should be of help to you in overcoming the obstacles you're likely to encounter.

INTERNATIONAL APPLICANTS

Foreign-born applicants are increasingly seeking positions in the United States, particularly in medicine. People who come from abroad sometimes encounter problems when seeking a position—sometimes it's an accent that puts off an interviewer, or a concern that the applicant's English isn't what it should be. Other times, it's no different from any other bias—the interviewer neglects to put you at the top of the list simply because he relates more strongly to applicants who are more like himself.

Although it will not be admitted, many interviewers see some international graduates as strange. You may come from a culture that is drastically different from that of the interviewer, and anything from your mannerisms to your accent may distance you from the interviewer.

However, keep in mind that many internationally born people have tremendous success in seeking positions in the United States. More than 20 percent of positions in medicine are held by people who attended medical school outside of the United States. Knowing that many such applicants are very successful can help build your confidence. Of course, given that you have received an interview, you must possess the necessary credentials. However, there is sometimes a preference for American graduates—and you'll be competing against other foreign graduates, as well—so it's important that you be prepared for the contest.

Because it's more difficult for U.S. administrators and physicians to glean what they need to from foreign letters of recommendation and transcripts, excelling in your interview becomes more important than ever. Keep an open and optimistic outlook to help display that you are the best candidate for the position.

Using Documents to Your Advantage

Strong letters of recommendation can help set a positive tone for your application and subsequent interview. If you have worked or studied in the United States, try to get letters of recommendation from previous American employers or professors. These letters carry more weight.

Unfortunately, letters from a foreign country may not be as helpful as you might like. A survey of 120 directors of residency in internal medicine (published in *Academic Medicine,* vol. 66) revealed that 73 percent of them considered letters of recommendation from a foreign country to be useless. Because of cultural differences, letters written by foreigners are often brief and emphasize characteristics that are valued in the applicant's culture but not necessarily in the United States. They also often lack a description of the applicant's professional and personal traits (both positive and negative). These are elements that are important to have in letters of recommendation.

For physicians applying for residency, your medical school transcripts may be examined carefully. Because foreign grading systems and courses may not be easily understood by an American interviewer, ask if he or she had any questions about your transcript, or if you should explain anything about your course work. This will offer you the opportunity to point out how your medical school experience relates to the job for which you are applying.

Talking the Talk

If you are not totally comfortable with English, the biggest hurdle for you may be the language barrier. (Don't worry, you're not alone. Most international applicants have not resided in the United States or other English-speaking countries. Or, if they have, they may still have a heavy accent and might not be proficient in the subtleties of American vernacular.)

Though you may find handling an interview in English difficult, both in speaking and in understanding the interviewer, it will be easier if you relax as much as possible. Show the interviewer that you can handle stress (i.e., the interview) with ease and that you will cope with living in the United States.

During the interview, don't be afraid to ask the interviewer to repeat herself. If you don't understand the question, simply ask the interviewer in a polite tone, "Excuse me, could you explain that a little more?" It is better to have the interviewer repeat the question than to try to answer it without an adequate understanding of what is being asked. In addition, do not hesitate to repeat yourself if you think that the interviewer has not understood what you have said. Remain calm throughout. Don't become impatient or aggravated if the interviewer cannot understand you or comments on your accent. Simply respond that you are aware of your accent and that you are going to learn more in the future in order to alleviate the problem, but that it has not been much of an obstacle in the past. A little humor may also soften an awkward moment.

One good reason not to worry unduly about your ease with the language is that interviewers frequently place less emphasis on fluency of English than many applicants believe. Also, according to a report in *Academic Medicine,* vol. 68, it has been found that the best predictor of success in residency training for internal medicine for an international applicant is not proficiency in English; rather, what is considered valuable is recent clinical experience. (This is followed in importance by scores on standardized tests.) As more facilities become aware of this recent study, an increasing number of interviewers may continue to de-emphasize the importance of the applicant's ability to speak fluent English.

Walking the Walk

If you can work around potential communication problems that may arise due to your lack of fluency in English, you will do fine during your interview. Always keep in mind that you are qualified to receive the position. Some further advice we have includes:

1. If the interviewer mispronounces your name, do not correct him unless he asks for help. Above all, do not become impatient or irritated if your name is mispronounced. If the interviewer does defer to you for pronunciation help, tell him in an affable manner, and thank him for being considerate and asking you for a correct pronunciation.
2. Do not dwell upon your place of origin during the interview. You may come from a very exotic location and be eager to talk about it with others. Now is not the appropriate time. If the interviewer asks you where you are from, tell him in a pleasant manner, but be very brief and answer only the question posed. Again, your primary goal is to present yourself as a flexible person with superior credentials and to show your commitment to making a success of your future.
3. Your manner of dress should be as close as possible to the average U.S. applicant. You may come from a place where people do not normally wear Western style suits, but you probably should do so for the interview. See chapter 3 for details concerning the preferred interview attire.
4. Do not attack or criticize U.S. culture. You may come from and advocate a political system that is very unlike that in the United States. However, you will not be doing yourself any favor by discussing this point now. If you are asked what you think about U.S. culture, focus on the strengths that you see. Emphasize the similarities between your culture and U.S. culture. For example, you could mention that both cultures place much significance on the family unit and a strong work ethic (these are true for most cul-

tures). If pressed on the issue, you might want to say simply that you are not the best person to make such comments as you have not lived here long enough to judge.
5. Don't beg for the position or demean yourself in any manner. In some cultures it may be acceptable to present yourself as subordinate to the interviewer in order to receive a position. However, this strategy will not likely succeed in the United States, and may cause the interviewer to lose respect for you or view you as unsubstantial.
6. Focus on your credentials. Discuss in detail past jobs and educational experience that you have. Your experience and relevant skills will be what wins the position for you. However, do not boast about your accomplishments. Some Americans have an incorrect preconception that international graduates have a tendency to brag. You do not want to fulfill their negative stereotype.
7. Make good eye contact. This is seen as a positive quality in this culture. It is not viewed as being disrespectful.
8. If you are taken to lunch, watch your table manners. Some people in the United States do not realize that behaviors that may be unacceptable here may be acceptable in other cultures. For example, burping may be permissible in your culture, but is regarded with distaste in the United States. Similarly, many cultures do not always use table utensils. Thus, be sure that you are aware of and practice appropriate U.S. table manners. Likewise, avoid showing offense at the table manners of others.
9. Do not argue with the interviewer to display that you are assertive. Some international graduates have the misconception that Americans view them as meek; however, exhibiting assertiveness is not necessary and may make you appear aggressive.
10. Be relaxed. Many international graduates are tense and think that they have to act in a very serious manner in order to be considered for a position. However, this seriousness is not needed. You may have to work extra hard to develop rapport with the interviewer. Try to let your sense of humor and warmth show if possible to facilitate rapport.
11. Do not ask about salary during the first interview.
12. If asked about your weaknesses, confess that your accent or weak English is probably your most prominent weakness. Outline a few

steps that you intend to undertake to enhance your English. However, also discuss steps that you have already taken to improve your English.
13. Do not be overly solicitous to the interviewer.
14. Be polite and kind to the secretaries and other staff members with whom you have contact.
15. Talk about your adaptability. The interviewer wants to offer a position to someone who will fit in effortlessly and get along well with everyone. As an international graduate, you may have resided in many different places and lived in a multitude of disparate cultures. If you have been successful in making these transitions, you will probably be able to do so here. If possible, discuss how you have been able to acclimate to other places and describe what lessons you have learned in the process.
16. Make sure that your visa is in order. For instance, in order to enter a U.S. residency program, an international graduate must either be a naturalized citizen, hold a permanent or temporary visa, or obtain a federal work permit. Before your interview, find out what you need to do so that you can accept a position in the United States. The interviewer may ask you whether you have resolved this issue, and it's important that you have done so. Do not make the interviewer think that it is going to be troublesome for him or her to give you the position.

Overall, the interviewer will grant you a positive evaluation if he or she thinks that you could do as good a job as any other American candidate. The interviewer wants someone who will be hardworking, levelheaded, and stable. If you can show that you possess these traits, you will do well. If hired, keep up the hard work. You want to make sure that you receive a good letter of recommendation from all of your employers.

Why Medicine? (Culturally Speaking)
You may be asked by an interviewer to discuss the reasons why you have chosen to go into medicine or a particular subspecialty. This question can be challenging for an international

graduate. Some answers that are suitable in a foreign culture may be met with disdain in the United States. For example, you may want to go into medicine because you come from a distinguished family that has produced many doctors. Generally, in America, personal choice is emphasized. Therefore, an interviewer usually wants to hear the personal reasons that you chose your field. For instance, a person in academia can describe the love she or he has always had for learning about certain topics. Answering this question skillfully is very important.

SPECIAL ℞ FOR SPECIAL POPULATIONS

In general, the social system that is currently in place in the United States is one that helps ensure that persons with minority status are not unfairly discriminated against when applying for a placement. However, this situation still does not guarantee that applicants with this status will receive the position they desire. To help overcome any possible barriers:

- Present yourself very professionally in the interview.
- At some point, address what you feel may be worrying the interviewer (perhaps the attendance record of a person with a disability or the difficulty with English for a foreign applicant).
- Stress your conscientiousness, your willingness to work hard, and your strong qualifications for the job.
- If you need some type of visa or special permit before taking a job, be sure that you have it prior to the interview. You don't want to give the interviewer an excuse not to hire you.
- If you are concerned that you may encounter discrimination, read the following chapter. If you feel you have been discriminated against, contact your local chapter of the American Civil Liberties Union.

18

FIELDING THE "UNASKABLE": WHAT TO DO WHEN YOUR INTERVIEWER ASKS YOU STRANGE OR ILLEGAL QUESTIONS

"Where were your parents born?"
"An eighteen-month-old, how nice. Do you plan on having more children?"
"Are you Chinese or Japanese?"
"Will you be preparing a big Christmas dinner?"

Heard in no particular context, these sound like general questions that might come up in a friendly conversation. However, should these questions arise in a job interview, they are actually illegal, and you have the right to choose how fully you answer them.

One of the difficult aspects of these unaskable questions, however, is that as the applicant, you walk a fine line. If an interviewer is intent on a subtle form of discrimination and is prying into territory he or she shouldn't be, then you'd prefer to be on your toes and not answer those questions. However, if the interviewer is also a mother of young children, her question about having more children may be nothing more than a way to identify with you and get to know you better. There might even be a similar innocence in the objectionable-sounding

"Chinese/Japanese" question if the interviewer is about to embark on a trip to either country.

With luck, you'll always encounter interviewers who are well aware of the treacherous territory of asking questions that are too personal or illegal; but if they're not, here's our advice on how best to handle them.

About the Job Discrimination Laws

Basically, most of these inappropriate questions are in violation of Title VII of the Civil Rights Act of 1964, which prohibits discrimination in selection based on race, color, religion, sex, or national origin. Additionally, amendments to this act in 1972 and 1981 have supplied further protection. Your state may also have laws that protect you.

If you encounter an interview situation where you feel you were discriminated against, contact the local chapter of the American Civil Liberties Union. They can help you determine what you want to do next.

IT CAN START IN THE VERY BEGINNING

The application form itself may have some unlawful questions, including the following:

1. **Name.** You do not have to give previous names, such as a maiden name, so long as the name you are using is your current legal name. Also, social titles (e.g., Mr., Mrs., Miss, Ms.) do not have to be supplied.
2. **Marital status.** You do not have to say whether or not you are married, nor do you have to divulge any information about where your spouse works or how many children you have.
3. **Gender.** Applicants do not have to specify their gender on the application.

4. **Height and weight.** These questions might be used primarily against people who are obese. No matter what your size, you needn't provide this information.
5. **Age and birth date.** You are only required to give this information if there are certain age requirements for the job. (This might apply in a non-medical job for something like bartending, since in some places you have to be at least 21 to serve alcoholic beverages. In a case such as this, you may even have to provide proof that you meet this age requirement.)
6. **Race.** This can be left blank on your job application. And in your interview, you do not have to answer questions that are aimed at ascertaining racial identity (e.g., "Are you originally from South America or Spain?" or "Where were you/your parents born?"). You needn't provide an interviewer with this information.
7. **Education.** Questions about education are inappropriate if they are unrelated to the position for which the applicant is applying. Obviously, for a medical job, a basic level of training (i.e., an M.D. or D.O.) is required and must be documented.
8. **Disabled status.** Any questions about whether you are disabled are unlawful. However, if your status may prevent you from fulfilling the requirements of the job, interviewers do have a right to know this information.
9. **Drug or alcohol abuse.** This is private information and should not be a part of your job application file.
10. **Photographs.** The organization cannot require that you provide a photograph with the application, though they may request one. Deciding whether to send a photograph is a judgment for each applicant to make.

AT THE INTERVIEW

The interview situation is more problematic. Interviewees are in a "want to please" mood, and it's difficult not to feel compelled to answer all the questions. The stress of the interview may also lead you into answering a question that you might recognize as inappropriate if you had more time to think about it.

One dilemma you'll face is trying to assess why certain questions are being asked. Some interviewers may bring up a topic that seems inappropriate but may actually not be meant that way. For example, an interviewer may ask an applicant if she is married. This question is sometimes a mere formality and may be meant to break the ice and get to know the interviewee better. Or if the doctor interviewing you loved being in the military service and sees something about the fact that you were in the service, he may ask where you were stationed, how you liked it, and when you left. This line of questioning doesn't mean he's trying to find out the circumstances of your discharge; it's more likely that he's reminiscing and enjoying himself. If you refuse to answer questions during the interview, he may be upset (and a bit embarrassed that you would think he was asking something improper) and hold it against you.

So, to answer or not to answer? That is the question. *Although these questions may be unfair, refusing to answer them may lead to disqualification for the position for which you have applied because you will be labeled difficult.*

At any rate, here are the topics that have been deemed off-limits for discussion in job interviews:

1. **Religion.** Questions concerning your religion are inappropriate. Should you encounter a question about your religious denomination, religious affiliation, church, parish, pastor, or what holidays you observe, the interviewer is out of place. And while, of course, you will be asked for references, it cannot be specified that one of them come from a member of the clergy.
2. **Pregnancy.** Interviewers may not ask about past, present, and future intended pregnancies. This includes pregnancies of female interviewees as well as pregnancies of spouses or significant others of male interviewees.
3. **Sexual orientation.** Whether you prefer men or women is an improper question.
4. **Military service.** Questions about the type of discharge received (e.g., dishonorable versus honorable) cannot be asked.
5. **Memberships.** Names of clubs to which the applicant belongs do not have to be provided by an interviewee.

6. **Possessions.** You needn't reveal whether you own a car or whether you own or rent your own home or apartment.
7. **Arrests.** Applicants do not have to provide information about arrests that did not lead to a conviction. Normally, however, an applicant does have to provide information about arrests that did actually lead to a conviction. And as you can certainly understand, an agency that is interviewing for a physician has the right to know that an applicant was convicted of rape.

We advise that you *needn't* answer these questions. However, if they are posed to you, here are some strategies that may save you from a blatant "I'm not going to answer that" reply:

Skirt the issue. "My spouse and I have only been married a year, and it's really much too early for us to talk about children. I don't know what we'll decide about that . . ."

Distract them. You might send the conversation another direction by asking a question of your own ("Before we talk about that, I'd appreciate it if you'd fill me in a little more about _____."). You may find that the interviewer doesn't have the nerve to re-ask the question.

Overall, we recommend that you be courteous to the interviewer and answer every question except those questions which you find objectionable. You should probably answer a question if you feel that it is not being asked for purposes of discrimination.

SEXUAL HARASSMENT

The problem of sexual harassment has been in the news a great deal lately, and experts have begun to examine the devastating effects such abuse can produce on employees.

No profession is immune from the problems of sexual harassment, and there is always the possibility you may encounter it when applying for medical positions. Interviewers are in a position of strength over applicants since they will be participating in the hiring decision, and this certainly offers an opportunity for misuse of power.

A study of 180 students who had recently completed residency interviews (published in the *Journal of the American Podiatric Association*) reported that 15.5 percent of participants experienced some form of sexual harassment (defined as unwelcome sexual attention) during the interview process! The sexual harassment included acts such as staring or leering, lewd and inappropriate sexual comments or jokes, and subtle sexual hints or pressures. In addition, subjects who had been harassed were asked what they thought would happen if they reported the harassment. The most frequently indicated responses were:

1. I would be labeled a troublemaker and be treated unfairly by others (36 percent).
2. I would no longer be considered for the program (32 percent).
3. Nothing would happen (29 percent).

As can be seen, even very educated people are afraid to report sexual harassment.

In addition, sexual harassment can be of a more subtle nature. For example, the University of Missouri-Columbia School of Medicine recently conducted a study on gender bias. The findings revealed that among 150 candidates to the School of Medicine, 34.0 percent of females were asked about their plans for having children. Conversely, only 8.7 percent of males were asked the same question. Obviously, many interviewers were assuming that females may decide to get pregnant and potentially drop out of medical school. In contrast, there was much less concern that males might withdraw prematurely from medical school if their significant other became pregnant.

What You Can and Should Do

Many people respond to sexual harassment during an interview by either displaying tolerance and ignoring the behavior (hoping that the behavior will discontinue) or turning the job down if an offer is made. You may not have to suffer by enduring this mistreatment or losing the job opportunity simply because one person is abusing his or her power. Fighting back against the harasser may not be an uncomplicated task, but confronting the problem may ultimately lead to a more acceptable resolution for you.

If you encounter obvious sexual harassment during an interview, you should react immediately. First, you should make it clear to the harasser during the interview that his or her behavior is making you uncomfortable. If the harassing behavior continues, discuss the matter with the harasser's immediate supervisor. If necessary, you may have to lodge your complaint with higher officials to bring the matter to a satisfactory conclusion. Use your judgment concerning such issues. However, you should not think that this situation was your fault or was caused by you in any way.

Until enhanced education and communication occurs, this exploitation will likely endure in our society and applicants need to know how to address the problem.

The ℞ for Staying Away from Strange or Illegal Questions

- Even a job application form may contain questions that you needn't answer. If something bothers you (like giving your race or your weight), leave it blank.
- If a question seems odd or inappropriate, try to assess why it's being asked. If the interviewer is a new father and asks if you have kids, it may be for the most innocent of reasons (his own excitement over having a baby).
- While you have the right to refuse to answer any question, that approach may not go over well with interviewers.
- To avoid an odd question without having to say you won't answer it, try skirting the issue or distracting the interviewer by bringing up another topic.
- If you feel the question is being asked for discriminatory reasons, you may want to call the local chapter of the American Civil Liberties Union for advice on how to proceed.
- Obvious sexual harassment should be reported to the interviewer's supervisor after warning the interviewer by indicating that he or she is making you feel uncomfortable.

19

THE POLITICS OF THE INTERVIEW

Ideally, after the interview process is complete, the best candidate should receive the position. However, ascertaining who the best candidate may be is a subjective procedure, and much politicking may occur behind the scenes. Everyone who has input into the hiring or admission process may have different ideas about who to hire. What happens when people disagree? How is a final decision made? It isn't easy.

A LITTLE BACKGROUND

Politics became a part of the process long before you came on the scene. In fact, the entire concept of establishing a search or admission committee involves a great deal of politics. People are chosen to serve on such a committee for a variety of reasons. Sometimes departmental representation is the most important. Other times, powerful people within the organization request to be on these committees so that they can have some influence over the type of candidate chosen. There's no telling how any given committee with which you interview is chosen, so from the start you're working with variables you can't anticipate or control.

For example, you may do an outstanding job during a medical faculty position interview. However, if one of the other applicants received his M.D. from the same university as the department chair, this applicant may have an advantage over you. This advantage could come about because the department chair has promised his old friend at the medical school that he'd do what he could for this "promising young man," or it could be as simple as the fact that the department chair really warmed to the fellow because he reminded him of himself as a young doctor. What's more, the department chair will probably not directly say that he wants this applicant hired, but may tell a few key players in the department how wonderful he thinks this candidate is. Based on this information, the pendulum may slowly swing in favor of this "promising young man" from the department chair's alma mater.

Now, keep in mind that doctors, administrators, and executives don't get together knowing how the politics will be played. If they all gravitate toward one candidate, then everyone is happy, and the best candidate gets hired. If not everyone is in agreement, the politics can be played a variety of ways, depending on how the committee and the various departments line up. If one particular committee member is truly the most powerful in this organization, then his candidate will almost certainly get hired. However, if three search committee members align against one modestly powerful committee member, then it is likely that the three-against-one odds will win out.

In other words, one reason why you shouldn't worry about the politics is that it's out of your hands. If you assume one person has the most power and try to curry favor, your plan might actually backfire. What if you end up snubbing someone who historically has always had a lot of say over who gets hired? Or what if you overpraise someone whom you assume is powerful but is actually greatly disliked by other departments? These factors may cause others to vote against you, simply because you were trying to play into what you assumed were the politics of the situation.

AGE-OLD SUCCESS STRATEGY: DO YOUR BEST

The only strategy you can use is to play up your strengths and present yourself in such a way that it is clear to those doing the hiring that you'll fit in and be an asset to their organization.

EQUAL OPPORTUNITY?

Politicking sometimes works against members of a minority group, but it also can benefit them. For instance, to meet government guidelines, certain groups may be preferred for a particular job. For example, an organization that needs to hire a social worker may determine that they do not have enough minority employees, so they may predetermine that they want to hire a minority female, despite the fact that the job will be advertised as open for all applicants and described as an equal opportunity position. However, based on preferential need, a qualified Caucasian male candidate may be excluded from consideration. This type of decision is not based exclusively on experience and credentials, but may be necessary to help maintain equality in the workplace.

If you do not receive a position to which you applied primarily due to politics, don't let it bother you too much. Politicking occurs in every hiring and admission decision, and sometimes it will work for you and sometimes it may work against you.

The ℞ for Playing Politics

- Don't worry too much about the politics. If you try to second-guess what's going on, you may play the game improperly and offend someone who could have been important to you.
- Learn the strategies that work for a good interview, and your hard work and persistence will inevitably pay off.
- When you lose a job, don't give up. If you've made a good impression and another opening comes along, then your hard work may pay off sooner rather than later.

20

AFTER THE INTERVIEW PROCESS IS OVER: "THE JOB IS YOURS!" OR "NEXT!" MOVING ON WHEN A PARTICULAR JOB FALLS THROUGH

The application is in, the job interviews are over, you've visited and liked the facility ... What happens next? What if you don't hear? Can you call them?

It's perfectly all right to follow up occasionally. Simply call and inquire whether a decision has been made about the position, and if it has not yet been decided, ask when it might be. This gives you the next date for a follow-up. (Wait a few days after the date given so that they have a little breathing space.)

At some point you'll have a definite answer. If it's good news, then the time has come to talk specifics. Ask about a starting date, and anything they'd like to have you attend to before arrival. Also inquire about who will explain job benefits to you.

This is also the time for any salary negotiations that need to take place. If you went back for a second round of interviews, then in all likelihood you've received basic information as to salary. If you're applying for your first job, then the amount isn't likely to be negotiable (though you might get the facility to pick up moving expenses, if they haven't already offered). Job applicants with prior work experience and senior staff members may be able to do a little more negotiating. Ask with whom you should speak about salary specifics, then start the discussion from there.

The Good News/Bad News Dilemma
"I got offered a position, but I haven't yet heard from the facility that is my first choice. What do I do now?"

Call the facility which is your first choice, and ask what the status of their job search is. While you can't hold them hostage over it, you might indicate that you've had another offer but would prefer to work for them. With luck, the person with whom you're speaking will give you an idea of whether or not the situation looks good for you.

"BETTER LUCK NEXT TIME"

If you don't get a job offer right away, don't be discouraged. You're in good company. No matter what your field or your level of education or expertise, there are almost always a good number of other qualified candidates applying for the same position. Chances are you won't get the first job for which you apply.

Many of the rejects for a particular job are terrific, well-educated, well-qualified people like yourself who for some reason just weren't the first choice for that particular job. As we've discussed, the chemistry may not have been right, the medical director's nephew may have gotten the job, or you may have lacked a specific type of experience that was important at this facility.

Your job now (and the true test of your character) is to pick yourself up and give it another try. Specifically, maintain the contacts that you have already made during the interview process. Call up people with whom you have interviewed (even those at a facility that has just filled a particular opening), and ask them to keep you in mind for other positions that may arise. If an interviewer has thought well of you, and you stay in touch, they may recommend you to others who have positions to fill. *In many cases, it really is who you know that determines whether you obtain a job.*

**Being Passed Over for a Residency
or Specialty Training Program**

Missing out on obtaining a position at this stage can be very discouraging. If you learn from the match program that you have not received a position, visit your medical school placement staff right away. They may be able to find an opening for you at another facility; it may not be as geographically desirable, but it is advisable to try to get some type of placement if you can.

If it's just too late, then you'll need to apply again at the next opportunity. This can be difficult, because often the schools accept applications just once a year. However, the key is to use the interval to your advantage, so that you'll have an improved outcome the next time.

- Ask a colleague or professor to look over your application packet. Get feedback from as many different people as possible.
- Request that someone help you rehearse for an interview.
- If you lack research or practical experience, approach a faculty member and express interest in becoming a member of his or her research team.

Finally, you can also call the directors of the programs where you failed to be accepted and ask for feedback on why you were rejected. They may be too busy to reply in detail, but they'll often try to carve out a few minutes to give you some idea of what happened. What you learn may help you feel better about not getting in. For example, if the director tells you that the program received 50 applications and admitted 5 residents, you may not feel as bad because the rejection wasn't personal, it was circumstantial.

"DUST YOURSELF OFF AND START ALL OVER AGAIN"

If you find yourself starting the process over again, here are the points you need to remember:

1. Each interview you have will be unique, so it's important that you obtain as much information as possible about each new interview situation. Never feel that you can coast through an interview without advance preparation.
2. The interview should be a dialogue between the interviewer and the interviewee, so be sure to think through questions to ask.
3. Keep in mind these general pointers that interviewees often forget when they are nervous:
   - get plenty of sleep the night before
   - dress nicely
   - be on time
   - show the interviewer respect
4. Be open, friendly, and honest during the interview. The interviewer is trying to get to know you and your skills better, and generally, the more open and straightforward your communication, the better you are likely to do.
5. Be kind and well intentioned to all whom you meet. If you do accept the position, you may be working there for many years. You want to make a good impression so that your future colleagues will like you immediately and that your transition will be smooth.
6. During the interview, collect information that will enable you to decide whether to reject or accept an offer.
7. Relax as much as possible. It is human nature to be nervous or feel threatened during times of stress, but you don't want to be so nervous that you can't think clearly. Speaking clearly and in an even tone during your interview will help reduce your anxiety.
8. Have some fun with the experience. It can be enjoyable to talk about yourself to someone who is attentive and interested in you.
9. Consider the interviewer. Is he or she bored? If so, speak a little faster or speak about a more exciting topic.

10. Remember that the interviewer is a person much like yourself. She or he probably wants the interview to go smoothly and wants to impress you. Both of you have a common goal—deciding if you are the best person to fill a given position. Once you can envision yourself as being on the same team as the interviewer, your interview will go well.

Finally, remember that being interviewed is hard work, and don't be surprised if you are far more prepared than the interviewer. One candidate recalls an interview in which the faculty member spent an entire half hour asking him, "So, what other questions do you have?" Fortunately, he was prepared and able to ask many questions, and the interview was successful.

Many people have argued that the personal interview is the single most important ingredient in receiving a medical position. Good luck with your interview!

APPENDIX A:
Preparing a Strong Curriculum Vitae

Your curriculum vitae (c.v., or résumé) is another important aspect of the application process and should be included with every application you submit.

Your c.v. is the one document that includes all of your accomplishments and credentials, and it needs to be neat and concise and do its best to sell who you are.

Here are the most common questions that arise about a c.v., and following these questions are three sample c.v.'s; one is a typical student c.v. (a student applying for a doctoral program in clinical psychology). A faculty c.v. is included as well.

WHAT DO I INCLUDE?

Include all relevant work experience, and outline your educational background after high school, including additional professional education you've received, such as major conferences attended. Include all committees and organizations to which you belong. Also incorporate information concerning research projects, clinical work, and publications or conference presentations you have done. Finally, add a section detailing volunteer or charity work you have done to display your altruistic nature.

HOW LONG SHOULD MY C.V. BE?

A c.v. should be as long as necessary. Many people feel compelled to make their c.v. as long as possible to impress the interviewer, and they include many things that are not important or even relevant (e.g., high school accomplishments). What an interviewer wants is what he or she really needs to know about you. For a med student, that information may be summed up in a single page. Yet a 10-page document listing work experience and publishing credits may be necessary for a physician who is applying for a faculty position.

Remember, too, that most interviewers have to read many, many applications, so it's important that your c.v. be highly readable and that you eliminate extraneous material. You want to hold the interviewer's attention long enough to make certain they have found the most important points.

IS THERE A PREFERRED FORMAT?

Refer to the sample c.v.'s. The key to a good c.v. is clarity and conciseness. Set it up so that an interviewer can quickly skim the document and still get a good idea of your qualifications. In addition, we recommend that you print your c.v. on a laser printer and use a good quality paper. If you can't do this yourself, take your résumé to a print shop. It may cost extra money, but it will be worth it in the long run. It's important that your c.v. look good.

HOW MUCH WORK DOES AN ACTIVITY HAVE TO REQUIRE BEFORE I INCLUDE IT ON MY C.V.?

Don't exaggerate your accomplishments. Include only projects, jobs, or organizations in which you were very active. As a general rule, don't include any activities to which you have devoted less than 25 hours. Often, students have participated in many research projects or volunteer organizations and did not actually do much work. For example, you may help a professor on a research project by helping hand out questionnaires in a college class. Does this count as a research activity? No, of course not. You don't want to be caught in a bind if the interviewer asks you to elaborate.

Before your interview, review your c.v. so that you will know the contents well. Be prepared to discuss any information contained in it.

(student example)

CURRICULUM VITAE

PERSONAL INFORMATION
Name: Donald R. Reynolds
Address: 3408 Ashe St.
Philadelphia, PA 10989
(569) 555-3098
Birth: June 24, 1970
Marital Status: Single

WORK EXPERIENCE
1993–94   Day care coordinator; Play Land Day Care, Philadelphia, PA

EDUCATIONAL BACKGROUND
B.A. Summa Cum Laude, Psychology, University of Pennsylvania, 1994.

RESEARCH EXPERIENCE
1992–Present   Research assistant to Dr. Mark Doctor, University of Pennsylvania, and research project on verbal abilities in children with autism.

CLINICAL EXPERIENCE
1993–94   Assessment and crisis management with teenagers in crisis, Peer Counseling Hotline, University of Pennsylvania.

SERVICE EXPERIENCE
1992–93   Psi Chi chapter president, University of Pennsylvania

HONOR SOCIETIES
Phi Kappa Phi
Psi Chi, National Honor Society of Psychology

MANUSCRIPT SUBMITTED FOR PUBLICATION
Doctor, M., and D. R. Reynolds, "An examination of verbal abilities in children with severe autism."

RESEARCH PRESENTATION
Reynolds, D.R., and M. Doctor, (May 1994). *Autism: New Frontiers.* Paper presented at the meeting of the Eastern Psychological Association, Newark, NJ.

John Smith
1234 Any St.
Anytown, MO 56789
(123) 555-7890

Objective: To obtain state-of-the-art training in neurology.

Education:
Sept. 1988   Bachelor of Arts, University of Kansas

Experience:
07.95–Present   Transitional Year Medicine, Department of Medicine, University of Michigan School of Medicine, Ann Arbor, MI.
07.94–06.95   Residency Training, Department of Psychiatry, University of Michigan School of Medicine, Ann Arbor, MI.
09.93–06.94   Research Assistant/Extern to Jacob Stiles, M.D., Assistant Professor and Staff Physician, SUNY Health Sciences, VA Medical Center, Syracuse, NY.
12.91–08.93   Clinical Rotation, Department of Intensive Care and Poison Control Center, Jouriles Postgraduate Medical Center, Chicago, IL.
05.91–11.91   Internship, Department of Internal Medicine, Jouriles Postgraduate Medical Center, Chicago, IL.
11.90–05.91   Internship, Department of Surgery, Jouriles Postgraduate Medical Center, Chicago, IL.

CURRICULUM VITAE

Mary Smith
22 Ridge Dr.
Anytown, MO 65203
(573) 555-2111
(573) 555-1122 (fax)

PERSONAL DATA

Place of Birth: Long Beach, California
Date of Birth: July 16, 1962

EDUCATION

Residency: Psychiatry
University of Kansas Medical Center
Lawrence, Kansas 1993–96
Medical School: University of Kansas Medical School
M.D. with Honors, 1989
Undergraduate: Kansas State University
Manhattan, Kansas
B.S. with High Honors, 1985

ACADEMIC ACHIEVEMENTS

M.D. with Honors, University of Kansas
Alpha Omega Alpha, Treasurer, University of Kansas
Summa Cum Laude, Kansas State University
Liberal Arts Honors Scholarship
President, Student Government, Kansas State University
Phi Kappa Phi

PROFESSIONAL EXPERIENCE AND SKILLS

Residency Training Highlights:
  Outpatient geropsychiatry
  Outpatient/inpatient dual diagnosis evaluation and treatment
  PRIME-MD; outpatient primary care consultation, liaison and
    education resident
  Psychopharmacology and individual psychotherapy in a managed
    care environment

Psychiatric Consultant (7 hours/week)
   Lenawee County Community Mental Health, Adrian, MI (1994>)

Contract Psychiatric Physician (after-hours coverage, 45 hours/month)
   Department of Veterans Affairs Medical Center
   Battle Creek, MI (1994>)

Wing Flight Surgeon (Primary Care Provider)
   Training Air Wing Two
   Kingsville, TX (1991–93)
     Scope of Responsibility:
        Provided primary medical care to 1,200 service members and their families
        Advised Air Wing Commander on all medical aspects of operational readiness and safety
        Supervised medical staff of the Aviation and Military Medicine Departments, consisting of an occupational health nurse, physician assistant, and 18 hospital corpsmen
        Initiated and supervised the clinic reorganization which resulted in increased patient census, satisfaction, and wing operational readiness
        Organized and provided medical services for Air Wing and Squadron Detachment to Virginia Beach, Key West, and aboard USS John F. Kennedy

ADMINISTRATIVE AND COMMITTEE ASSIGNMENTS

Department of Psychiatry, University of Michigan Medical Center
   Facilitator, Resident Board Review Course (1995>)

Department of Veterans Affairs Medical Center, Ann Arbor, MI (1995>)
   Drug Seeking Behavior Committee

Training Air Wing Two and Naval Hospital Branch Clinic
   Naval Air Station, Kingsville, TX (1991–93)
     Disaster Management and Emergency Medical Services Coordinator
     Chairman, Base Suicide Prevention Committee
     Drug and Alcohol Advisory Council
     Resuscitative Medicine Training and Liaison Officer
     Medical Quality Assurance Committee
     Aviation Mishap Investigation Board
     Field Naval Aviator Evaluation Board
     Human Factors Board

CURRENT PROFESSIONAL ACTIVITIES

American Medical Association
American Psychiatric Association
Michigan Psychiatric Society
Alpha Omega Alpha Honor Medical Society

MEDICAL LICENSURE CERTIFICATIONS

American Board of Psychiatry and Neurology, eligible, June 1996
Virginia, 56007, 1990>
Texas, J0910, 1992>
Michigan, 4301061489, 1994>
Diplomate, National Board of Medical Examiners, 374803, 1990
Federal DEA Number, available on request

APPENDIX B:

HELPING OTHERS: ANSWERING THE ULTIMATE QUESTION, "HOW DO I GET INTO MED SCHOOL?"

Once you become a doctor, you will gain popularity in social situations for several reasons, among them:

1. People will want to describe their symptoms (or those of a friend) to you with the hope that you'll give them a little medical advice to "tide them through until Monday."
2. They'll want some suggestions on how they can get their relatives or son or daughter (or themselves) into medical school.

While you'll soon become an expert at finessing your way through social conversations about a person's latest rash or back pain, we thought it might be helpful to have some of the following suggestions about getting into medical school.

WHAT TO TELL ASPIRING DOCTORS

Getting into medical school is quite challenging today, particularly with the recent reduction in residency slots. This will have a trickle-down effect on medical school admissions, and candidates of the future will have to be particularly sharp to get in.

Just as in getting a job, the interview for medical school is key—as a matter of fact, it may be the single most important hurdle in the race for admission, so when you talk to candidates stress to them that their interview is very important and that winging it is unwise.

WHO GETS INTERVIEWS?

Only a select few applicants are going to gain admission to a specific medical school, and the school will only interview candidates who they feel are fully qualified.

To determine whether a candidate gets an interview, the admissions committee will be looking at:

1. grades
2. course work
3. Medical College Admission Test (MCAT) scores
4. letter of intent; personal statement
5. letters of recommendation

For a candidate to get through the first admissions hurdle, this package must be a strong one.

Here are a couple of additional recommendations you might make to aspiring doctors at this stage:

1. Participate in volunteer work to demonstrate devotion and an altruistic nature.
2. Participate in any research opportunities that are offered by your school or anywhere else.

Both these efforts display motivation, a willingness to work hard, and a desire to learn beyond the classroom—attributes that are important in becoming a doctor.

Once the candidate gains an interview, he or she should feel quite pleased. The admissions committee has determined that this person has the basic credentials to be a student there. Now it's the candidate's task to convince the admissions committee that there is no one else who deserves that seat!

Here's the advice to give that hopeful candidate:

Practice good interview skills ahead of time. Trade off with other premed students and work together doing mock interviews. If you can find someone who recently went through the process to critique you, that's all the better.

Read about the school before you arrive. Many schools have a general philosophy that you should understand in advance of the interview. What you need to know is generally contained in the application packet.

Come to the interview with a basic understanding of the health care system. The health care system is a complicated one, but it is important that anyone who aspires to be a doctor have a basic understanding of the situation today.

Don't expect medical decisions to be black and white. If you've been premed in college then you've already learned that medicine is not a clear-cut science. While certain illnesses can be neatly diagnosed and treated, others are less clear and the answers are ambiguous. Future doctors need to be knowledgeable, but they also need to be able to tolerate ambiguity.

ADVICE ON ACING THE INTERVIEW

The interview process itself generally involves two separate interviews with two representatives from the school. One will be a physician, and the other will likely be a person from the basic sciences (e.g., physiology, anatomy, biochemistry, microbiology). There may also be an interview with a current student of the school; tell your candidate not to relax—the student's opinion can sometimes influence the decision.

Among the general questions a candidate should be prepared to answer are the following:

1. What skills do you possess that will help make you a good physician?
2. Tell me about yourself.
3. Why are you interested in going into medicine?
4. Why are you applying to this medical school?
5. What will you do if you don't get into medical school?

Candidates will also likely be asked if they intend to specialize. Until recently, the trend was toward specialization; but now, with the increasing openings for general practitioners in HMOs, the current tendency is for more students to want to become family physicians, internists, and pediatricians. If a candidate has made up his mind, he should certainly feel free to say so. However, if he's not yet sure, it's all right to indicate that as well.

At the interview, tell your candidate to observe the following:

Be friendly. As with anything else, if the interviewers like you, they will be far more likely to want to help you out than if you've arrived with a chip on your shoulder.

Display confidence without being cocky. This is an important attribute for a doctor who has to tell a patient what the best type of treatment is—and mean it.

Demonstrate compatibility. Schools want students who are going to fit in.

Show enthusiasm for medicine. While medicine is a field which, in the past, parents have often pressured their children to enter because of income and stability, it is important that you display that you have made the decision yourself and that your enthusiasm for medicine is certainly a compelling factor. Some of the best answers to questions about why you've chosen medicine as a career include:

1. I like science and have done well in this area. Medicine offers me the opportunity to continue with my interest.
2. I find it rewarding to help people, and becoming a doctor lets me fulfill this desire.
3. My aunt (or father or uncle) suffers from _____, and this caused me to get interested in medicine. I thought that Dr. _____, who treated her (or him), was an incredible person, and I wanted to be like him.
4. My mother (or any other close relative) is a physician, and I have always enjoyed hearing her talk about her work. Also, living with a doctor has sensitized me to the difficulties in this profession, and I think that I am well prepared because of this experience.
5. I like an intellectual challenge, and I know medicine will provide that.

6. I've always enjoyed reading about how the heart, brain, and body work, and I can't imagine a better place to continue to explore this interest.

Medical schools are looking for applicants who have superior intellectual ability, character, integrity, leadership qualities, and the ability to be unflappable under stress. Try to think which of these characteristics are your strong suit and come up with ways that you can express these strengths in the interview. Anecdotes about personal experiences generally work best. (For example, you might tell of a time when something significant happened: When you were 15 a cousin went into the ocean too far and became frightened. You had the presence of mind to swim out and pull him in.)

When it comes to any weaknesses, don't blame others. Maybe a bad grade in one class really was because of a terrible professor, but med school admissions people are often turned off by someone who blames others. You can refer to the difficulty with the professor, but then tell an anecdote about how you usually can overcome this type of problem. Or if the poor grade can be explained by the fact that you were suffering from mononucleosis, be open about your bout with the illness.

Remain neutral when it comes to emotionally charged topics. Euthanasia, treatment of AIDS, and abortion are just a few of the issues that can spark heated discussions among any population, and most certainly among doctors. Expressing some of the pros and cons of each issue is a good way of not having to take a specific stand (which may not be the same as the interviewer's). If an interviewer pushes for an opinion, you might comment that every case is different and you would take things on an individual basis; another good answer is to say, "A medical education will undoubtedly change the way I think about things, and I'd prefer to reserve judgment until the future."

Ask questions and take notes. To show that you are interested, ask questions about the school and what your future would be like there. A sampling of some appropriate questions would include:

1. What medical facilities exist for medical students' rotations?
2. Are there research opportunities for medical students? What are some of the projects going on now?

3. Do any faculty members do research or specialize in _____?
4. What kind of work do students do with faculty members?
5. What aspects of this university helped you decide to come here and have impelled you to stay? (Smile when you ask this question, and pose it modestly.)

AN IMPORTANT "WHY" AND "WHAT"

The question "Why are you applying here?" provides you with the opportunity to explain why you are a perfect fit for the school, and it may be the most important question you'll be asked. Here are guidelines:

1. Talk about distinctive qualities of the school—the quality of the teaching or expertise in a field (cardiovascular) that particularly interests you.
2. Comment on the uniqueness of the school and how it applies to you.
3. Discuss what you know about the school that really appealed to you.

"What if you don't get in?" This may seem like a somewhat tactless question, but it's also a way that an interviewer can learn more about your dedication. The applicant who replies, "I guess I'll go to law school" can forget about a career in medicine. The applicant who says, "I'll do what I can to bolster my chances for the following year" has just increased her or his odds of not having to wait.

AND IF YOU REALLY DON'T GET IN . . .

Many qualified applicants won't get in, simply because there is a shortage of openings. Tell your candidate to take a critical look at his or her package. Retaking the MCAT tests or beefing up a not-strong-enough academic record by adding some important courses may help. You might also recommend that your aspiring doctor/candidate look into volunteer work or research for the coming year to help strengthen the application. In this field, persistence and dedication often pay off.

The ℞

1. Only qualified applicants receive an interview, so if a candidate is asked to come for a visit there is already reason for optimism.
2. A candidate should do some homework about the school and know the faculty's interests and specialties.
3. A candidate should educate him- or herself about the structure of the health care system.
4. He or she should be as neutral as possible about touchy subjects such as AIDS, abortion, or euthanasia.
5. A candidate should show that he or she is confident, but should avoid bragging or appearing arrogant.
6. By discussing volunteer work, a candidate can show altruism.
7. A candidate should show enthusiasm for medicine, not just the perks (e.g., money, prestige).
8. Good candidates will demonstrate character and integrity. Being honest and not exaggerating is a good example of a way to do this.
9. If a candidate is not admitted during this round, he or she should remain optimistic and reapply.

SELECTED RESOURCES

2. The Basics of Interview Prep

Brandt, L. J., and L. Pousada. (1990). "Interviewing in the 1990s—The Hard Cell versus the Soft Cell." *New England Journal of Medicine* 323:838.

Edis, M. (1990). *Both Sides of Selection*. Basingstoke, Eng.: MacMillan Education.

Loretto, V. (1986). "Recruitment: Effective Interviewing Is Based on More Than Intuition." *Personnel Journal,* 65:100–107.

Robin, A. P., T. Bombeck, R. Pollak, and L. M. Nyhus. (1991). "Introduction of Bias in Residency-Candidate Interviews." *Surgery,* 110:253–258.

Stringer, S. P., N. J. Cassisi, and W. H. Slattery. (1992). "Otolaryngology Residency Selection Process: Medical Student Perspective." *Archives of Otolaryngology Head and Neck Surgery.* 118:365–366.

Yate, M. J. (1991). *Knock 'Em Dead with Great Answers to Tough Interview Questions*. Holbrook, Mass.: Bob Adams.

3. Looking Good on the Outside: Acknowledging the Importance of Appearance

Bardack, N. R., and F. T. McAndrew. (1986). "The Influence of Physical Attractiveness and Manner of Dress on Success in a Simulated Personnel Decision." *Journal of Social Psychology,* 125:777–778.

Dion, K. K., E. Berscheid, and E. Walster. (1972). "What Is Beautiful Is Good." *Journal of Personality and Social Psychology,* 24:285–290.

Hanger, T. I. (1991). "Presenting Yourself Successfully." *Nursing,* 21:87–88.

Snyder, M., E. D. Tanke, and E. Berscheid. (1977). "Social Perception and Interpersonal Behavior: On the Self-Fulfilling Nature of Social Stereotypes." *Journal of Personality and Social Psychology,* 35:656–666.

Yate, M. J. (1991). *Knock 'Em Dead with Great Answers to Tough Interview Questions*. Holbrook, Mass.: Bob Adams.

4. The Basic Interview

Anderson, K. (1991). "Making a Good First Impression." *Nursing,* 21:145–146.

Hanger, T. I. (1991). "Presenting Yourself Successfully." *Nursing,* 21:87–88.

5. "A Group Interview with How Many?" What You Need to Know for a Panel Interview

Fish, J. (1992). "How to Respond at Interview." *British Journal of Nursing,* 1:252–255.

———. (1992). "Preparing for an Interview." *British Journal of Nursing,* 1:201–204.

7. The Ultimate Secret to the Successful Interview: Paying Attention to the Interviewer

Medley, H. A. (1978). *Sweaty Palms: The Neglected Art of Being Interviewed.* Belmont, Calif.: Lifetime Learning Publications.

8. Getting Started: Internship/Residency Interviews

DeLisa, J. A., S. S. Jain, and D. I. Campagnolo. (1994). "Factors Used by Physical Medicine and Rehabilitation Residency Training Directors to Select Their Residents." *American Journal of Physical Medicine and Rehabilitation,* 73:152–156.

Galazka, S. S., G. E. Kikano, and S. Zyzanski. (1994). "Methods of Recruiting and Selecting Residents for U.S. Family Practice Residencies." *Academic Medicine,* 69:304–306.

Lebovits, A., J. E. Cottrell, and C. Capuano. (1993). "The Selection of a Residency Program: Prospective Anesthesiologists Compared to Others." *Anesthesiology and Analgesia,* 77:313–317.

Simmonds, A. C., IV., J. M. Robbins, M. R. Brinker, J. C. Rice, and M. D. Kerstein. (1990). "Factors Important to Students in Selecting a Residency Program." *Academic Medicine,* 65:640–643.

Stringer, S. P., N. J. Cassisi, and W. H. Slattery. (1992). "Otolaryngology Residency Selection Process: Medical Student Perspective." *Archives of Otolaryngology Head and Neck Surgery,* 118:365–366.

11. Surviving the Managed Care Interview

Curtiss, F. R. (1989). "Managed Health Care." *American Journal of Hospital Pharmacy,* 46:742–763.

Moretto, T. J. (1988). "How Joining an HMO or PPO Can Benefit Your Practice." *Indiana Medicine,* 81:1033–1034.

Offner, E., and H. B. Zacker. (1996). "Understanding Different Models of Health Maintenance Organizations." *Current Opinions in Pediatrics,* 8:171–175.

Wilbur, D. L. (1971). "HMO—Health Maintenance Organization." *Postgraduate Medicine,* 50:177–178.

12. *"So You Want to Teach?" Faculty Position Interviews*

Levendusky, P. G. (1986). "The Clinical Job Interview: From the Ivory Tower to the Real World." *Behavior Therapist,* 9:11–12.

Lineham, M. M. (1983). "Interviewing to Get the Job." *Behavior Therapist,* 6:3–4.

Paunonen, S. V., D. N. Jackson, and S. M. Oberman. (1987). "Personnel Selection Decisions: Effects of Applicant Personality and the Letter of Reference." *Organizational Behavior and Human Decision Process,* 40:96–114.

13. *Go to the Head of the Class: Directorship Interviews*

Bencivenga, G. (May 1994). "Job Hunting? How Well Can YOU Answer These 64 Tough Interview Questions?" *TWA Ambassador* (advertisement).

Bostwick, B. E. (1981). *111 Proven Techniques and Strategies for Getting the Job Interview.* New York: John Wiley & Sons.

Gilmore, D. C., and G. R. Ferris. (1989). "The Politics of the Interview." In *The Employment Interview: Theory, Research, and Practice,* edited by R. W. Eder and G. R. Ferris, 195–203. Newbury Park, Calif.: Sage.

Medley, H. A. (1978). *Sweaty Palms: The Neglected Art of Being Interviewed.* Belmont, Calif.: Lifetime Learning Publications.

Morton, G. M. (1964). *The Arts of Costume and Personal Appearance.* New York: John Wiley & Sons.

Yate, M. J. (1994). *Knock 'Em Dead: The Ultimate Job Seeker's Handbook.* Holbrook, Mass.: Bob Adams.

———. (1991). *Knock 'Em Dead with Great Answers to Tough Interview Questions.* Holbrook, Mass.: Bob Adams.

15. *"I didn't Say That, Did I?" Mistakes People Make When Interviewing*

Edis, M. (1990). *Both Sides of Selection.* Basingstoke, Eng.: MacMillan Education.

16. Advoiding the Sweaty Palms Syndrome: Managing Your Anxiety

American Psychiatric Association. (1994). *Diagnostic and Statistical Manual of Mental Disorders*. 4th ed. Washington, D.C.: American Psychiatric Association.

Craske, M. G., D. H. Barlow, and T. O'Leary. (1992). *Mastery of Your Anxiety and Worry*. Albany, N.Y.: Graywind.

Meichenbaum, D. (1975). "A Self-Instructional Approach to Stress Management: A Proposal for Stress Inoculation Training." In *Stress and Anxiety*, edited by I. Sarason & C. D. Speilberger. Vol. 2. New York: John Wiley & Sons.

———. (1985). *Stress Inoculation Training*. New York: Pergamon.

17. Special Tips for Special Situations: Overcoming Possible Obstacles

Gayed, N. M. (1991). "Residency Directors' Assessments of Which Selection Criteria Best Predicts the Performances of Foreign-Born Foreign Medical Graduates during Internal Medicine Residencies." *Academic Medicine*, 66:699–701.

Klesges, R. C., M. L. Klem, C. L. Hanson, L. H. Eck, J. Ernest, D. O'Laughlin, A. Garrott, and R. Rife. (1990). "The Effects of Applicant's Health Status and Qualifications on Simulated Hiring Decisions." *International Journal of Obesity*, 14:527–535.

Larkin, J. C., and H. A. Pines. (1979). "No Fat Persons Need Apply: Experimental Studies of the Overweight Stereotype and Hiring Preference." *Social and Work Occupations*. 6:312–327.

Part, H. M. and R. J. Markert. (1993). "Predicting the First-Year Performance of International Medical Graduates in an Internal Medicine Residency." *Academic Medicine*, 68:856–858.

Rao, N. R., A. E. Meinzer, and S. S. Berman. (1994). "Perspectives on Screening and Interviewing International Medical Graduates for Psychiatric Residency Training Programs." *Academic Psychiatry*, 18:178–188.

Tagalakis, V., R. Amsel, and C. S. Fitchen. (1988). "Job Interview Strategies for People with a Visible Disability." *Journal of Applied Social Psychology*, 18:520–532.

18. Fielding the "Unaskable": What to Do When Your Interviewer Asks You Strange or Illegal Questions

Loretto, V. "Recruitment: Effective Interviewing Is Based on More Than Intuition." *Personnel Journal,* 65:101–107.

Stiffman, M. N., and M. D. Blake. (1991). "The Effect of Applicants' Gender on the Content of a Medical School's Admission Interview." *Academic Medicine,* 66:629.

Wizer, D. R. (1992). "Sexual Harassment in Podiatric Medical Education: The Residency Interview Process." *Journal of the American Podiatric Association,* 82:590–593.

Yate, M. J. (1991). *Knock 'Em Dead With Great Answers to Tough Interview Questions.* Holbrook, Mass: Bob Adams.

Appendix B: Helping Others: Answering the Ultimate Question, "How Do I Get into Med School"

Powis, D. A., T. Bristow, T. C. Waring, and D. L. O'Connell. (1992). "The Structured Interview as a Tool for Predicting Premature Withdrawal from Medical School." *Australian and New Zealand Journal of Medicine.* 22:692–698.

Index

Academic Medicine, 82, 87, 177, 178
adaptability, 181
administrators, 95
adult sensibilities, displaying, 84
advertisements
 answering, 25–26, 35
 for directorships, 124
 of HMOs, 106
 in professional journals, 10
advice, asking for, 72–73
African Americans, 176
age, illegal questions about, 185
AIDS, 92, 213
alcohol abuse, illegal questions about, 185
American Civil Liberties Union (ACLU), 182, 184
American Journal of Physical Medicine and Rehabilitation, 77, 83
American Medical Association, 77
anxiety, 4
 during interviews, 14, 57
 speech patterns and, 16–17
 see also stress
appearance, 23–33
 of application forms, 26–27
 of cover letters, 23–26
 personal, 27–30 (*see also* clothing)
application forms, 26
 illegal questions on, 184–85
application process for residencies, 78–81
appropriateness, sense of, 154
Archives of Otolaryngology Head and Neck Surgery, 21
arrests, illegal questions about, 187

assertiveness, displaying, 128–29
 by international applicants, 180
athletic activities, informal interviews during, 68
attending physicians, 3, 91–98
 interviews for, 93–96
 researching positions for, 91–93
attire, *see* clothing

Barlow, D. H., 161
bedside manner, 148
bias, 15, 171–72
 against foreign born, 176–82
 gender, *see* gender bias
 against obese, 174–76
 against physically disabled, 172–74
birth date, illegal questions about, 185
board certification, 89, 108
 oral exams for, 141–49
body language, 37–38, 60
bragging, 153–54
breathing
 deep, 161
 during muscle relaxation exercise, 164
Brinker, M. R., 86–87

Campagnolo, D. I., 77
Career Mosaic's Health Care Connection, 11
case managers, 109, 110
case presentation, 147–48
catastrophizing, 161
chiefs of staff, *see* medical directors
Civil Rights Act (1964), 184

clear speech, 16–18
  during oral exam, 143
clothing, 3, 27–29
  for directorship interviews, 137–38
  disheveled, 155
  for international applicants, 179
  for lunch interviews, 63, 64
  obesity and, 175
colloquium, 117–19
Columbia School of Medicine, 188
committee responsibilities, 94
community
  expressing interest in, 46–47
  faculty positions and, 119
  group practices and, 103
  positive attitude toward, 44
  researching, 19–20
compatibility, demonstrating, 82–83, 212
competence, conveying, 116–17
complaints
  about other interviews, 44–45, 71
  about supervisors, 157
  about travel, 43–44
computers
  application forms on, 27
  medical directors and, 129
  preparing cover letters on, 24
confidence, conveying, 117, 156, 212
  during oral exam, 142
coping methods, 161–69
costs, interview-related, 21–22
  for faculty position applicants, 121
  for residency applicants, 78
cover letters, 23–26
  directorship, 124
  for faculty position applications, 114
Craske, M. G., 161
credentials, 116–17
  of international applicants, 180
credibility, 117
criminal record, questions about, 187
cues, interviewer's, 37–38
  at lunch, 65

curriculum vitae (c.v.), 2, 4, 23, 201–7
  for directorships, 124
  example of, 203–7
  for faculty position applications, 114, 117
  format for, 202
  length of, 201–2
  sending out, 10
  what to include on, 201

deans, medical school, 123
delegation of responsibilities, 130–31
DeLisa, J. A., 77
department chairs, 123
  and politics of interviews, 191–93
desensitization, 166
desperation, avoiding appearance of, 156
directorships, 123–39
  cover letters for, 124
  gender bias and, 138
  interviews for, 126–38
  researching, 125
disabilities, 172–74
  illegal questions about, 185
discrimination, 171–72
  illegal questions and, 183–89
  racial, 176
drinking, 185
  at lunch interviews, 66
drug abuse, 185

eccentricity, 155
education, illegal questions about, 185
emotionally charged topics, neutrality about, 213
English, lack of fluency in, 178–79, 180–81
enthusiasm, conveying, 83–84, 154–55, 212
  by obese people, 175
expenses, *see* costs
eye contact, 37, 58, 71, 180

faculty, medical school, 3, 113–21
  interviews for, 115–20
  letters of recommendation from, 80–81
  screening process for, 114
fear hierarchy, 166
fellowships
  beginning job hunt during, 10
  interviews for, 89
  financial discussions, 157–58
flexibility, need for
  in group practices, 102
  in HMOs, 109–10
foreign-born applicants, 4, 176–82
formularies, 109–10

gatekeepers, 106
gender bias, 138
  illegal questions and, 184–85
  sexual harassment and, 187–88
golf course, informal interviews on, 68
grants, ability to secure, 116–17
grooming, 3
group practices, 3, 99–104
  affiliations of, 100–101
  being an asset to, 103–4
  researching, 19
  types of, 99–100
  what to look for in, 102–3
gum chewing, 30

haircuts, 3, 29
Halo or Horn effect, 15
handshake, 36, 58
health care reform, 103
health maintenance organizations (HMOs), 3, 105–10
  benefits of, 106–7
  group practice affiliations with, 100, 103
  interviews with, 108–10
  researching, 19, 107–8
height, illegal questions about, 185

hobbies, 50–51
honesty, 41
hospital practices, 100
hosts, overnight, 53
hygiene, 155

illegal questions, 4, 183–89
immune system, impact of stress on, 160
innovative ideas, 132
insurance plans, 101
  see also health maintenance organizations
intent, letters of, 79, 210
international applicants, 4, 176–82
International Journal of Obesity, 174
Internet, 11, 19
internships, *see* residencies
interviews, 2–4, 35–55, 198–99
  arriving on time for, 31–33
  for attending physicians, 93–96
  clothing for, 27–30
  confirming, 30–31
  cues in, 37–38
  developing rapport during, 41–43
  for directorships, 126–38
  ending, 51–52
  for faculty positions, 115–19
  for fellowships, 89
  first moments of, 36–37
  follow-up on, 195
  for group practices, 101–2
  honesty in, 41
  informal, during athletic activities, 68
  landing, 7–12
  listening during, 45–46
  mealtime, *see* lunch interviews
  medical school, 209–15
  mistakes made during, 153–58
  naturalness in, 39–40
  panel, 57–62, 127
  paying attention during, 69–73
  politics of, 191–93
  preparation for, 13–22, 168

for residencies, 77, 82–86
sexual harassment during, 187–89
showing respect during, 38–39
silences during, 40
thank-you notes for, 54, 59, 61
see also questions, interview

Jain, S. S., 77
Joint Commission of Accreditation of Hospital Organizations (JCAHO), 129
jokes, offensive, 156
Journal of the American Medical Association, 19
Journal of Applied Social Psychology, 172
journals, professional, 10, 19, 107
see also specific journals

Kerstein, M. D., 86–87
Knock 'em Dead with Great Answers to Tough Interview Questions (Yate), 15, 25

Larkin, J. C., 174
letterhead stationery, 24
letters, 10
of intent, 79, 210
of recommendation, 80–81, 154, 177, 210
licensing, 11, 102
listening skills, 45–46
during panel interviews, 59
loans
from family members, 22
student, 21
lunch interviews, 63–68
clothing for, 63, 64
conversation during, 66–67
drinking at, 66
food to order for, 65
for international applicants, 180
"mad about me" syndrome, 153–54
mail, applying by, 23–26

managed care, 7, 8
see also health maintenance organizations
marital status, illegal questions about, 184
marketing yourself, 8–9
Mastery of Your Anxiety and Worry (Craske, Barlow, and O'Leary), 161
meals, *see* lunch interviews
Medical College Admission Test (MCAT), 210, 214
medical directors
attending physicians interviewed by, 93–94
see also directorships
medical school
and attending physician applications, 94
applying for residencies during last year of, *see* residencies
costs of applying to, 21
deans of, 123
faculty of, *see* faculty, medical school
foreign, 177–78
getting into, giving advice on, 209–15
placement staff of, 197
and politics of interviews, 191–92
medical societies, 104
MEDLINE, 107
Meichenbaum, Donald, 166, 167
memberships, illegal questions about, 186
military service, illegal questions about, 186
minority groups
and politics of interviews, 193
see also biases
Missouri, University of, 188
multiple specialty clinics, 100
mumbling, avoiding, 17
muscle relaxation, *see* progressive muscle relaxation

name on application form, 184
name-dropping, 116

National Association of Physician Recruiters, 8
National Residency Matching Program, 78
negativity, avoiding, 43–45, 71, 157
nervousness, 156–57
  see also anxiety
networking, 10
newspapers, 20
  as source of conversational topics, 66–67
notebook, job-hunting, 3, 9
  for residencies, 79
nurse practitioners, 109
Nursing, 36

obesity, 174–76
  illegal questions and, 185
off-color language, avoiding, 17
O'Leary, T., 161
online job search, 11
oral exams, 3, 141–49
  case presentation in, 147–48
  patient interviews in, 145–46
  video analysis in, 147
Organizational Behavior and Human Decision Process, 116
organizational skills, 84–85, 130
overnight guests, 53

panel interviews, 57–62
  for directorships, 127
  survival tips for, 59–60
paperwork
  of attending physicians, 94
  of group practices, 101
patient care, 96
  in HMOs, 106
patient interviews, 145–46
performance review, 110
personal statement, 79
personnel offices, 11, 14
phobias, stress-induced, 160
photographs, requests for, 185
physical disabilities, *see* disabilities

Pines, H. A., 174
politics
  avoiding discussions of, 155–56
  international applicants and, 179
  of interviews, 191–93
positive attitude
  projecting, 43–45, 157
  to reduce stress, 168–69
positive reinforcement, 72
possessions, illegal questions about, 187
preferred provider organizations (PPOs), 105–8
pregnancy, illegal questions about, 186
  gender bias and, 188
prejudice, *see* bias
primary care physicians, HMO, 106
profanity, avoiding, 17
professional journals, 10, 19, 107
progressive muscle relaxation, 162–65
  desensitization and, 166
  stress inoculation training and, 168
publications, 94, 114, 116–17
  tenure and, 120

questions, interview
  appropriateness of responses to, 154
  for attending physicians, 93–95
  "big three," 15–16
  for directorships, 132–33, 135–37
  for faculty positions, 118–19
  illegal, 4, 183–89
  about interests, 50–51
  listening to, 45–45
  panel, 58–60
  for residencies, 85
  standard versus fanciful, 14–15
  about strengths, 50
  variations in, 14
  about weaknesses, 47–49

racial discrimination, 176
  illegal questions and, 185
rapport, developing, 41–43, 128
  with international applicants, 180

recommendation, letters of, 80–81, 154
  for international applicants, 177
  for medical school, 210
recruitment firms, 8, 10–11
relaxation, *see* progressive muscle relaxation
religion
  avoiding discussions of, 155–56
  illegal questions about, 186
research
  experience in, 94, 210
  of faculty position applicants, 117
  fellowships for, 89
residencies, 3, 77–90
  application process for, 78–81
  beginning job hunt during, 10
  being passed over for, 197
  costs of applying for, 21
  cover letters for, 24
  international applicants for, 177–78, 181
  interviews for, 82–86, 187–88
  tour of site for, 86–87
  training provided during, 88
respect
  for examiner, 144–45
  for hospital staff, 95, 181
  for interviewer, 38–39
responsibilities
  adult, 84
  committee, 94
  delegation of, 130–31
Rice, J. C., 86–87
Robbins, J. M., 86–87

safe place, imaginary, 165
salary
  discussing, during interview, 157–58, 180
  negotiating, 195
self-monitoring, 167–68
sexual harassment, 187–89
sexual orientation, illegal questions about, 186

silence during interview, 40
Simmonds, A. C., 86–87
smoking, 30
Social and Work Occupations (Larkin and Pines), 174
speaking clearly, 16–18
  during oral exam, 143
specialties
  being passed over for training in, 197
  expertise in, 129
  for faculty positions, 114, 115
  job market for, 7
  managed care and, 106, 109, 110
  multiple, clinics for, 100
  qualifying oral exams for, 3, 141–49
  residencies and, 78
  staying current on, 20
state licensing boards, 11
stereotypes, 15
  of disabled, 174
strengths, talking about, 50, 153–54, 213
  of obese people, 175–76
  of physically disabled, 173
stress, 159–69
  behavioral symptoms of, 160
  cognitive symptoms of, 160–61
  desperation and, 156
  management of, 4, 161–69
  of international applicants, 178
  of oral exams, 144
  of overnight guests, 53
  of panel interviews, 127
  physiological symptoms of, 160
  travel-related, 44
stress inoculation training (SIT), 166–68
student loans, 21
subspecialties, 89

"taboo" subjects, 155–56
table manners, 65
  cultural differences in, 180
tennis court, informal interviews on, 68

tenure, 120–21
thank-you notes
   to interviewers, 54, 59, 61
   to overnight hosts, 53
time cues, 38
tours of facilities
   for faculty position applicants, 119
   for residency applicants, 86–87
traditional group practices, 99–100
training directors, residency, 82
travel, 30
   questions about, during interview, 43–44

video analysis, 147
visas, 181
Vocational Rehabilitation Act (1973), 172
volunteer work, 210

weaknesses, talking about, 47–50, 213
   of international applicants, 180–81
web sites, 11
weight, illegal questions about, 185
worrying, 160–61

Yate, Martin, 15, 25, 124

ABOUT THE AUTHORS

Javad H. Kashani, M. D. is professor and chief, division of psychiatry and neurology at the University of Missouri-Columbia. He is also professor of psychology and pediatrics and director of Children and Adolescents Services at Mid-Missouri Mental Health Center. His research in the area of internalizing disorders and family violence has led to the publication of over 100 scientific articles on the topic. His clinical studies in the last two decades merited him the most prestigious award in child psychiatry in North America—the Blanche F. Ittleson Award.

Wesley D. Allan is currently completing his Ph.D. in child clinical psychology at the University of Missouri-Columbia. His primary interest is child psychology research, and he has coauthored numerous journal articles and several books on the topic.